HAVE YOU EVER BURNED YOUR HAND MAKING POPSICLES?

DO YOU THINK AL DENTE INVENTED SPAGHETTI?

For two decades, *The Starving Students' Cookbook* has allayed the fears of even the most reluctant chefs. If cooking delicious, inexpensive meals and snacks with easy preparation and practically no clean-up sounds good to you, this is the only book you'll ever need. Before you know it, you'll be making:

Homemade Pesto Sauce · Cheap Roast · Shrimp Egg Foo Yung · Spinach Mandarin Salad ·
Tequila-Soaked Fish · Curried Chicken · Salade Niçoise · Beef Mexicana

These delicious creations plus over a hundred more will make your ventures into the kitchen happy ones. You'll never know how you lived without it.

"The instructions are so understandable and easy that any non-cook can make meals in minutes."

—Forecast

"One of the most elementary cookbooks ever devised. . . . This time and money saver can help inspire eating habits and nutrition for college students."

—Changing Times

"Although geared for the crowd, *The Starving Students' Cookbook* is useful for anyone who doesn't want to cook and doesn't want to learn to cook, but does want to eat."

—San Diego Union-Tribune

THE STARVING STUDENTS' COOKBOOK

THE STARVING STUDENTS'

COOKBOOK

DEDE HALL

WARNER BOOKS

An AOL Time Warner Company

Warner Books Edition

Copyright © 2002 by Patricia "Dede" Hall
All rights reserved.

This Warner Books edition is published by arrangement with
Warner Books Inc., 1271 Avenue of the Americas, New York, NY 10020

Visit our Web site at www.twbookmark.com.

An AOL Time Warner Company

Printed in the United States of America

First Warner Books Printing: July 2002

10 9 8 7 6 5 4 3 2 1

Library of Congress Cataloging-in-Publication Data
Hall, Dede.
    The starving students' cookbook / Dede Hall.—Rev. ed.; Warner Books ed.
      p. cm.
    Includes index.
    ISBN 0-446-67961-5
    1. Low budget cookery. I. Title.

TX652 .H327 2002
641.5'52—dc21
                                                    2002016813

Book design and text composition by Nancy Singer Olaguera
Cover design by John Valk
Illustrations by Mari Estrella

This book is dedicated
to my English (and Australian) families
Mark, Mandy, Alex, Calvin, Maisie,
Sally, Daren, Emma, Abby,
Stephen, Chris, Olivia, Nicole, Madeline
Love to you all.

COLLEGE STUDENTS!

Living on your own and trying to cut college costs is great, but why didn't someone tell you what a PAIN cooking for yourself can be? Now, at last, a way to ease your misery—a cookbook just for you with recipes that are EASY to follow, QUICK to make, 1 or 2 servings, LOW COST, and above all, GREAT TASTING!!

THE STARVING STUDENTS' COOKBOOK would probably make a gourmet cook shudder. This book is filled with recipe directions such as "splash," "squirt," "handful," even a "plop" or two. These descriptions are used simply to make cooking time faster and easier and won't change the good taste of the food.

You probably get your fill of studying every day and the last thing you want to do is "study" a cookbook. Wouldn't you like to have meals that taste good without having to work at it? Even if you have never cooked before, you can now.

THE STARVING STUDENTS' COOKBOOK is written just for YOU!

CONTENTS

THE EATING RIGHT PYRAMID

The U.S. Department of Agriculture recently publicized this visual guide in order to help the public become more aware of healthy choices in selecting their daily meals. The USDA's Dietary Guidelines state: "Each of these food groups provides some, but not all, of the nutrients you need. No one food group is more important than another; for good health, you need them all."

What Counts As 1 Serving?

The amount of food that counts as 1 serving is listed at the right. If you eat a larger portion, count it as more than 1 serving. For example, a dinner portion of spaghetti would count as 2 or 3 servings of pasta.

Be sure to eat at least the lowest number of servings from the five major food groups listed at the right. You need them for the vitamins, minerals, carbohydrates, and protein they provide. Just try to pick the lowest-fat choices from the food groups. No specific serving size is given for the fats, oils, and sweets group because the message is USE SPARINGLY.

FOOD GROUPS

Milk, Yogurt, and Cheese

1 cup of milk or yogurt	1½ ounces of natural cheese	2 ounces of process cheese

Meat, Poultry, Fish, Dry Beans, Eggs, and Nuts

2–3 ounces of cooked lean meat, poultry, or fish	½ cup of cooked dry beans, 1 egg, or 2 tablespoons of peanut butter count as 1 ounce of lean meat

Vegetable

1 cup of raw leafy vegetables	½ cup of other vegetables, cooked or chopped raw	¾ cup of vegetable juice

Fruit

1 medium apple, banana, orange	½ cup of chopped, cooked, or canned fruit	¾ cup of fruit juice

Bread, Cereal, Rice, and Pasta

1 slice of bread	1 ounce of ready-to-eat cereal	½ cup of cooked cereal, rice, or pasta

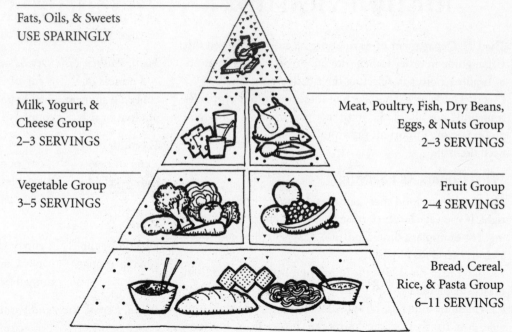

KEY

● Fat (naturally occurring and added)

▼ Sugars (added)

These symbols show fat and added sugars in foods. They come mostly from the fats, oils, and sweets group. But foods in other groups—such as cheese or ice cream from the milk group or french fries from the vegetable group—can also provide fat and added sugars.

Fats, Oils, & Sweets
USE SPARINGLY

Milk, Yogurt, & Cheese Group
2–3 SERVINGS

Meat, Poultry, Fish, Dry Beans, Eggs, & Nuts Group
2–3 SERVINGS

Vegetable Group
3–5 SERVINGS

Fruit Group
2–4 SERVINGS

Bread, Cereal, Rice, & Pasta Group
6–11 SERVINGS

SHOPPING TIPS & KITCHEN HINTS

In the Supermarket

Check prices against weight to find the best buy.

Buy small quantities when cooking for one. Large "economy size" is no bargain when you have to throw away spoiled food.

Buy fruit and vegetables in season: They'll cost less and taste better.

NEVER buy or use canned goods that have "puffed out" ends, as this is a sign gas has built up within the can, which could produce a potentially deadly toxin.

Do your marketing after you have eaten. You'll buy less "junk food" and spend a lot less money.

For sweeter, juicier oranges, look for smoother skin and heavier weight.

Large size in fruit and vegetables doesn't always mean quality.

When head lettuce is too costly, try using some of the various leafy types. You'll be pleased how delicious they are.

In the Kitchen

Keep fish in a tightly covered container to avoid a fishy smell throughout your refrigerator.

Roll lemons until slightly soft before squeezing. You will get a lot more juice out of them.

To chop onions without tears, hold a piece of bread partway in your mouth.

A paper towel in the bottom of the refrigerator vegetable drawer will keep the drawer clean and absorb food moisture.

Don't pour cold water into hot aluminum or stainless steel pans, it could cause them to warp out of shape.

Chopped apples, pears, and bananas won't get discolored if you squeeze a bit of lemon juice on them.

Don't forget: When using the garbage disposal, run a strong flow of cold water through it at the same time to prevent drain blockage.

Adding a few grains of rice to salt keeps moisture from forming in the shaker and helps salt to flow freely.

BASIC SUPPLIES TO GET YOU COOKING

Basic Utensils

Fry Pan (Skillet) and Lid
Plastic Bowl Set (with lids)
Pancake Turner (Spatula)
Glass Baking Dish (rectangle)
Large Ovenproof Pan and Lid
Saucepan with Lid
Aluminum Foil
Measuring Spoons
Sharp Knife
Glass Measuring Cup
Wooden Spoons
Scissors (to cut open stubborn packaging)

Don't Forget . . . Knife, Fork, Spoon, and a Can Opener!

Basic Ingredients: What to buy and where to find it in the supermarket

DAIRY CASE (always check freshness date):
    Eggs, Milk, Sour Cream, Margarine, Cheddar Cheese, Orange Juice

CONDIMENTS:
    Catsup, Mayonnaise, Mustard, Salad Dressing, Vegetable Oil, Vinegar, Lemon Juice, Barbecue Sauce, Soy Sauce

BAKING PRODUCTS AND SPICES:
    Salt, Pepper, Sugar (granulated, brown), Garlic Powder or Salt, Flour, Herbs and Spices—Basil, Dill Weed, Parsley, Curry Powder, Paprika

CANNED VEGETABLES AND FRUIT:
    Beans (refried, chili, pork & beans), Cup-up
    Tomatoes, Corn, Pear Halves, Peach Slices

SAUCES, SOUPS, AND GRAVY:
    Beef Gravy, Dry Onion Soup Mix, Tomato Sauce,
    Soup (condensed style)—Cream of Mushroom,
    Tomato, Chicken Noodle

MACARONI, RICE, AND MEAT PRODUCTS:
    Macaroni, Pasta, Rice (preferably not instant), Tuna

BREAD PRODUCTS AND SNACKS:
    Bread (your choice), Jelly or Jam, Peanut Butter,
    Pudding, Gelatin (Jell-O), Crackers, Cookies,
    Popcorn, Chips

These items will be useful if you have space in your
refrigerator.

FRESH PRODUCE:
    Fruit (in season), Carrots, Celery, Potatoes, Onions,
    Nuts

MEAT CASE:
    Hot Dogs, Fish Fillets, Ground Beef (hamburger),
    Chicken

FROZEN FOOD (if you have freezer space):
    Ice Cream or Frozen Yogurt, Chopped Spinach,
    Broccoli Spears, Peas

HANDY HINT

Know how to tell a hard-cooked egg from a raw one? The hard-cooked egg will spin like crazy.

❖

Adding a little vinegar to water when hard-boiling eggs helps prevent eggs from cracking.

❖

To check if an egg is fresh, place it in a bowl of salted water.
If it sinks, it's fresh; if it floats, throw it away!

BASICALLY BREAKFAST

1. FRIED:

1. Heat butter in skillet on medium high heat till sizzles.
2. Break eggs gently into skillet.
3. Reduce heat to medium. Then:
   SUNNY SIDE UP—cook just till whites are set.
   BASTED—add spoonful water to pan, cover, and let steam 2 minutes.
   OVER EASY—when whites are set, gently flip over with pancake turner.

2. SCRAMBLED:

1. Break eggs into bowl; beat with fork lightly.
2. Heat butter in skillet on medium high heat till sizzles. Pour eggs in.
3. Reduce heat to medium low. Cook and stir gently till done to your liking.

3. SOFT-COOKED:

1. Place eggs (with shells on) in saucepan. Add enough water to cover eggs. Set pan on stove and set heat at high.
2. When water begins to boil rapidly, start timing the eggs: 3 minutes for medium-done soft-cooked egg.
3. Crack shell at large end of egg and remove shell. Eat from shell or scoop into a small bowl.

4. HARD-COOKED:

1. Same as for soft-cooked, except boil 10 minutes.
2. Turn off heat and let eggs sit in pan till water is cooled.

Eggs—The Way You Like Them

5 Minutes
Serves 1

Basically Breakfast

Skillet, Bowl or Saucepan

Top of Stove

CORNED BEEF HASH

10 Minutes
Serves 1–2

Basically Breakfast

Large Skillet
Top of Stove
High Heat

NEED:

1 tablespoon VEGETABLE OIL
1 16-ounce can CORNED BEEF HASH
½ ONION, chopped
¼ GREEN BELL PEPPER, chopped
plop CATSUP
dash BLACK PEPPER

STEP 1: In large mixing bowl, dump together all ingredients and mix well.
STEP 2: Heat oil in large skillet on high heat. Add hash mixture and press flat with spatula or large spoon.
STEP 3: Cook until brown on underside and turn over. (The hash will probably fall apart, but keep turning it until nicely browned.)

*If you want to add a little zing, add some Tabasco Sauce.
Tastes fabulous with fried or scrambled eggs.*

NEED:
- 4 slices BREAD (couple days old)
- 2 EGGS
- 2 tablespoons MILK
- 2 tablespoons MARGARINE

STEP 1: Mix eggs and milk in pie pan.
STEP 2: In skillet, on medium high heat, heat margarine till hot. Dip bread slice into egg mixture, then lay onto hot skillet.
STEP 3: Cook each side till golden.

Top with syrup, applesauce, powdered sugar, or fresh fruit.

FRENCH TOAST

10 Minutes
Serves 1

Basically Breakfast

Pie Pan & Skillet
Top of Stove
Medium High Heat

Omelet Fillings
& Toppings

1 to 2 Minutes

Basically Breakfast

- Scoop of HOT CHILI and handful grated CHEESE
- Handful finely chopped HAM and SWISS CHEESE
- Sliced AVOCADO, finely chopped TOMATO, and GREEN BELL PEPPER
- MUSHROOMS, lightly cooked in margarine in skillet
- Spoonful SOUR CREAM and chopped PARSLEY
- Grated CHEESE, spoonful BARBECUE SAUCE, and ALFALFA SPROUTS
- Crumbled BACON, sliced BANANA

Be creative with your own combinations!!

Misc. Utensils

OMELET

10 Minutes
Serves 1

NEED:
3 EGGS
2 tablespoons MILK
dash SALT
tablespoon MARGARINE

STEP 1: In bowl, mix together eggs, milk, and salt.
STEP 2: In skillet, on medium heat, melt margarine. Add egg mixture. As eggs cook on edges, gently lift edges with spatula (flat spoon), pushing to center. Rest of uncooked egg will flow underneath cooked part. Do not stir, or you will have scrambled eggs.
STEP 3: When eggs are done to liking and surface is still moist, put any filling you want onto half of omelet and fold over. Cover with lid and cook 1 to 2 minutes or till eggs are golden on underside.

Basically Breakfast

Skillet With Lid
Top of Stove
Medium Heat

HANDY HINT

Catsup won't come out? Stick a straw through to bottom of bottle and remove. This lets in enough air to start the catsup flowing.

❖

Hamburgers in a hurry: Poke a hole in the middle of the hamburger patty when you shape it. The burger will cook faster and the hole will disappear when done.

QUICK LUNCHES

NEED:
  4 ENGLISH MUFFINS, cut in half
  1 8-ounce can TOMATO SAUCE
  Thin slices of any of the following:
      ONION, GREEN BELL PEPPER, MUSHROOMS, OLIVES,
      PEPPERONI, ANCHOVIES, SALAMI
  8 slices MOZZARELLA CHEESE

Preheat oven to 350°.

STEP 1: Spread each half English muffin with tomato sauce.
STEP 2: Add slices of any combination from above ingredients, ending with
         cheese on top.
STEP 3: Place on foil in 350° oven till cheese melts.

ENGLISH MUFFIN PIZZAS

15 Minutes
Serves 2–3

Quick
Lunches

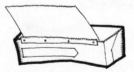

Aluminum Foil
350° Oven

French Dipped Cheese Sandwich

10 Minutes
Serves 1

Quick Lunches

Pie Pan or Shallow Dish

Skillet

Top of Stove

Medium High Heat

NEED:

1 EGG
1 tablespoon MILK
3 tablespoons BUTTER or MARGARINE
2 slices WHITE or WHEAT BREAD
1 slice CHEESE
1 slice BOLOGNA or COOKED HAM

STEP 1: In pie pan or shallow dish, beat together egg and milk with a fork.

STEP 2: Using some of the butter, butter 1 side of each slice of bread.

STEP 3: Place cheese and meat on buttered slice and press sides together. Dip sandwich into egg mixture, coating each side.

STEP 4: In skillet, on medium high heat, melt remaining butter. Cook sandwich until golden brown on each side.

Combine in small bowl, then spread in pita bread pocket:

½ of 3-ounce package CREAM CHEESE
1 tablespoon SOUR CREAM

Next, fill pocket with:

LETTUCE, shredded
1 TOMATO, thinly sliced
chopped BLACK OLIVES (spoonful)
FETA or RICOTTA CHEESE (couple spoonfuls)
sliced BANANA

GREEK PITA POCKET

5 Minutes
Serves 1

Quick Lunches

Small Bowl
No Cooking

ONION STACKS & HOME-MADE BARBECUE SAUCE

5 Minutes
Serves 1

Quick
Lunches

Small Bowl or Cup
Skillet
Top of Stove
Medium Heat

NEED:

¼ cup CATSUP
1 tablespoon BROWN SUGAR
½ teaspoon VINEGAR
1 tablespoon VEGETABLE OIL
½ ONION, sliced
½ GREEN BELL PEPPER, sliced
1–2 KAISER ROLLS, sliced in half lengthwise

HOME-MADE BARBECUE SAUCE: *In small bowl or cup, stir together catsup, brown sugar, and vinegar. Set aside to use in recipe.*

STEP 1: In skillet, on medium high, heat oil. Add onion and pepper slices. Stir and cook 3–5 minutes or until onion is golden.
STEP 2: Pour barbecue sauce over vegetables and stir. Turn heat to medium low and cook 3 minutes.
STEP 3: Spoon hot onions & peppers with sauce between sliced rolls.

Really cheap and really good!

NEED:

    1 8-ounce can PORK AND BEANS
    1 spoonful BROWN SUGAR
    1 plop CATSUP
    1 tablespoon chopped ONION
    dab MUSTARD

STEP 1: Stir all ingredients together in small saucepan. Cook on medium heat till beans start to boil.

STEP 2: Reduce heat to lowest setting. Cover. Cook 10 minutes to blend flavors.

Delicious served over toasted buns.

FANCY PORK & BEANS

....

10 Minutes

Serves 1

Quick Lunches

Saucepan With Lid

Top of Stove

Medium to Lowest Heat

Quick Sandwich Spreads

3 Minutes
Serves 1

Quick
Lunches

Small Bowl
No Cooking

CARROT & PEANUT BUTTER

¼ cup PEANUT BUTTER
1 tablespoon SUNFLOWER SEEDS, shelled
1 tablespoon RAISINS
1 small CARROT, shredded
1 teaspoon CREAM CHEESE, softened

Mix in small bowl and spread on bread or toast.

EGG & OLIVE

Mix together:
2 HARD-COOKED EGGS, chopped
1 1½-ounce can chopped BLACK OLIVES
1 teaspoon SWEET PICKLE RELISH
1 tablespoon MAYONNAISE

Good on egg bread.

PEANUT BUTTER, SLICED BANANAS, HONEY

Spread wheat bread with butter, honey, and peanut butter.
Lay bananas in middle.

CHEESE & ONION

½ ONION, thinly sliced
splash VINEGAR
dash PEPPER
SHARP CHEDDAR CHEESE, sliced

Lay onion in small bowl and sprinkle with vinegar and pepper. Let sit for a couple of minutes to blend flavors. Butter bread and layer with sliced cheese and onions.

CREAM CHEESE & PINEAPPLE

Mix together:
3-ounce package CREAM CHEESE, softened
1 tablespoon CRUSHED PINEAPPLE, well drained
1 teaspoon SUNFLOWER SEEDS

Good on raisin bread.

3 Minutes
Serves 2–3

Quick
Lunches

Small Bowl
No Cooking

HANDY HINT

For flavor variations in soup:
Use chicken, vegetable, or beef broth in place of some of the
water required when making soups.

SOUPS

NEED:

4 slices BACON, cut up before cooking
1 GREEN ONION, sliced thin
1 8-ounce can CREAM-STYLE CORN
1 can CREAM OF MUSHROOM SOUP
1 soup can MILK
1 raw POTATO, cut into ½-inch cubes
1 6-ounce can minced CLAMS and juice

STEP 1: In saucepan, on medium heat, cook bacon till almost crisp. Add onion. Cook 1 more minute. Carefully drain grease into an old can. (Discard grease later when solidified.)

STEP 2: In same pan, add rest of ingredients. Bring to a boil. Reduce heat to low. Cover. Cook, stirring often, till potatoes are done (approximately 15 minutes).

FULL MEAL
CLAM CHOWDER

20 Minutes
Serves 2–3

Soups

Saucepan With Lid
Top of Stove
Medium to Low Heat

Late-Night Chicken Soup

20 Minutes
Serves 1

Soups

Saucepan
Top of Stove
Medium to Low Heat

NEED:
1 10-ounce can CHICKEN BROTH
1 soup can WATER
2 teaspoons UNCOOKED RICE (not instant)
1 EGG
1 teaspoon LEMON JUICE

STEP 1: On medium high heat, into saucepan pour chicken broth, water, and rice. Bring to boil. Turn heat down to lowest setting. Cook 20 minutes.

STEP 2: Just before serving, beat egg with lemon juice and pour into soup. Stir with fork and cook 1 minute on lowest setting. Serve while hot.

When you are up all night studying, try this instead of coffee to pep you up.

POTATO SOUP

18 Minutes
Serves 1–2

NEED:

½ ONION, chopped small
1 tablespoon MARGARINE
2 medium POTATOES, peeled and chopped small
½ cup WATER
1 cup NONFAT MILK (not powdered)
SALT, PEPPER to taste

STEP 1: In saucepan, on high heat, cook onion in hot margarine till limp (approximately 2 minutes).

STEP 2: Add potatoes and water. Boil gently 15 minutes or till potatoes are soft. Mash potatoes with fork while still in water. Do not drain!

STEP 3: Add milk, salt, and pepper. Reduce heat to low and cook till hot, stirring often.

Soups

Saucepan
Top of Stove
High to Low Heat

Quick Minestrone Soup

15 Minutes
Serves 1–2

Soups

Saucepan With Lid
Top of Stove
Medium to Low Heat

NEED:

    1 tablespoon VEGETABLE OIL
    1 ZUCCHINI, chopped
    handful leftover COOKED MEAT, chopped small
    1 16-ounce can WHOLE TOMATOES, cut up
    1 8-ounce can GREEN BEANS (or 1 cup any leftover vegetables)
    1 can WATER (use empty tomato can)
    ½ envelope DRY ONION SOUP MIX
    small handful UNCOOKED MACARONI (small elbow)

STEP 1: In saucepan, on medium heat, heat oil and stir in zucchini and meat. Cook 2 minutes.

STEP 2: Add tomatoes, green beans, and water. Bring to a boil.

STEP 3: Stir in onion soup mix and macaroni. Cover and cook 10 minutes on low heat.

Very filling. Great on a cold night.

SNAPPY TOMATO SOUP

NEED:
  1 medium TOMATO, cut into quarters
  handful ONION, chopped
  1 small stalk CELERY, chopped
  1 11-ounce can TOMATO JUICE, CLAMATO, or V-8 JUICE
  couple squirts each TABASCO SAUCE and WORCESTERSHIRE SAUCE

STEP 1: Place tomato, onion, and celery into blender jar. Blend on high 1 minute or until almost soupy.
STEP 2: Pour mixture into saucepan. Stir in juice, Tabasco Sauce, and Worcestershire Sauce. Stir and bring to boil on medium high heat.
STEP 3: Turn heat to low (simmer). Cover and cook 10 minutes.

MANHATTAN STYLE CLAM CHOWDER

Use recipe as above adding to Step 2:
  1 8-ounce can chopped CLAMS, drained

10 Minutes
Serves 1

Soups

Electric Blender
Saucepan with Lid
Top of Stove
Medium High to Low Heat

25

Handy Hint

Cleaning head lettuce: Remove core by tapping it sharply on hard surface.
Core will come out easily. Then hold lettuce upside down under cold running water.
Cleans and separates leaves at the same time.

❖

To keep strawberries fresh longer, don't wash them until you are ready to use them.

SALADS

SALAD 1

NEED:

    ½ CUCUMBER, peeled and chopped
    3 tablespoons PLAIN YOGURT
    dash each of GARLIC SALT, PEPPER
    ¼ HEAD LETTUCE, shredded

Stir first 3 ingredients together in small bowl and serve over shredded lettuce.

SALAD 2

NEED:

    ½ CUCUMBER, peeled and sliced thin
    ½ small RED ONION
    ½ cup SOUR CREAM
    quick squirt VINEGAR
    dash each of GARLIC SALT, PEPPER

Mix all ingredients together in small bowl. Chilling before eating improves the flavor.

TWO CUCUMBER SALADS

5 Minutes
Serves 1–2

Salads

Small Bowl
No Cooking

Caprese Salad

3 Minutes
Serves 1

Salads

Salad Plate
Sharp Knife
No Cooking

NEED:
   ¼ pound FRESH MOZZARELLA CHEESE, cut into ¼-inch slices
   1 large TOMATO, cut into ¼-inch slices
   4 large leaves FRESH BASIL, cut up
   1 teaspoon OLIVE OIL

STEP 1: On plate, layer mozzarella cheese slices with tomato slices.
STEP 2: Sprinkle with fresh basil.
STEP 3: Drizzle olive oil over top.

NEED:

- 2 TOMATOES, thinly sliced
- ½ small RED ONION, thinly sliced
- SALT, PEPPER to taste
- ½ teaspoon DRY BASIL
- 1 tablespoon WINE VINEGAR
- 3 tablespoons OLIVE OIL (or VEGETABLE OIL)

STEP 1: In shallow platter, layer tomato and onion slices. Sprinkle with salt, pepper, and basil. Pour vinegar and then oil over salad.

STEP 2: Let salad sit for at least 10 minutes to allow flavors to blend.

FRESH TOMATO SALAD

10 Minutes

Serves 1–2

Salads

Shallow Plate or Platter

No Cooking

Hot Taco Salad

15 Minutes
Serves 1–2

Salads

Skillet
Top of Stove
Medium Low Heat

NEED:

1 8-ounce can REFRIED BEANS (check for a brand made without lard)
6–8 CHERRY TOMATOES, cut in half
¼ HEAD LETTUCE, shredded
handful shredded CHEDDAR CHEESE
couple handfuls TORTILLA CHIPS (or corn chips)

STEP 1: Heat beans in skillet on medium low heat till very hot.
STEP 2: Turn off heat. Add the rest of the ingredients. Stir gently.
STEP 3: Sprinkle more grated cheese on top and, if you need to save time and dishwashing, eat right out of the pan.

NEED:

    1 8-ounce can GREEN BEANS, chilled
    1 15-ounce can sliced NEW POTATOES, chilled
    handful SALAD GREENS
    2 TOMATOES, cut into quarters
    ¼ ONION, thinly sliced
    handful BLACK or GREEN OLIVES
    1 3-ounce can TUNA, drained well
    6 ANCHOVY STRIPS (optional)
    ¼ cup Oil & Vinegar Salad Dressing (your choice)
    1 HARD-COOKED EGG, quartered

STEP 1: Drain green beans and potatoes and set aside.
STEP 2: Dump salad greens into large salad bowl.
STEP 3: Lay on top of greens the tomatoes, onions, olives, tuna, anchovies, green beans, and potatoes.
STEP 4: Toss with salad dressing and top with hard-cooked egg.

This is not just a salad, it is a meal!!

NICOISE SALAD

30 Minutes
Serves 1–2

Salads

Large Salad Bowl
No Cooking

Pasta Salad

....

5 Minutes
Serves 1–2

Salads

Large Saucepan
(for cooking pasta)
Large Salad Bowl
Top of Stove

NEED:

1 cup COOKED PASTA SHELLS, well drained and cooled (great use for leftover pasta)
1 8-ounce can 3 BEAN SALAD, drained well
¼ RED ONION, thinly sliced
¼ GREEN BELL PEPPER, thinly sliced
1 TOMATO, chopped
handful MOZZARELLA CHEESE, cut into small cubes
ITALIAN SALAD DRESSING

STEP 1: Dump cooled pasta into large salad bowl.
STEP 2: Add beans, onion, bell pepper, tomato, and cheese cubes. Toss gently.
STEP 3: Add dressing (to your liking) and toss well.

Try experimenting with different ingredients—you really can't go wrong! I've even added cantaloupe, basil leaves, raisins, etc.

NEED:

SALAD GREENS
1 APPLE, peeled, cored, and cut into bite-size pieces
1 PEAR, cored and cut into bite-size pieces
small handful chopped ALMONDS, PECANS, or WALNUTS
BLACK PEPPER
CHUTNEY SALAD DRESSING (page 40)
handful of POPPED CORN (make sure it is *not stale*)

STEP 1: Dump salad greens into salad bowl.
STEP 2: Add apple, pear, nuts, and dash black pepper.
STEP 3: Toss salad with dressing (you decide how much to use).
STEP 4: Just before ready to eat, sprinkle popcorn on top.

You will love this salad, guaranteed!!

POPCORN FRUIT SALAD

3 Minutes
Serves 1

Salads

Salad Bowl

No Cooking

Spinach Mandarin Salad

5 Minutes
Serves 1–2

Salads

Salad Bowl
No Cooking

NEED:

1 small bunch RAW SPINACH (or small bag prewashed)
¼ raw JICAMA, peeled and cut into strips or small chunks (found in the fresh produce section of supermarket)
1 11-ounce can MANDARIN ORANGES, drained
SWEET AND SOUR FRENCH DRESSING (page 41)
6 MUSHROOMS, washed and sliced
1 HARD-COOKED EGG, sliced

STEP 1: If using bunch spinach, wash spinach well and pat dry with paper towels, then tear spinach into bite-size pieces.
STEP 2: Dump spinach, jicama, and oranges into large salad bowl.
STEP 3: Add dressing (amount according to taste) and toss gently.
STEP 4: Top with mushrooms and egg.

JICAMA *(pronounced hic-a-ma) is a crisp and delicious vegetable. Best when served cold and crisp. Use in salads or dip in Ranch Dressing.*

Salad Dressings

ITALIAN–Mix together and toss with salad

2 tablespoons VEGETABLE OIL
1 tablespoon VINEGAR or LEMON JUICE
1 small CLOVE GARLIC, mashed
dash each of SALT, PEPPER
pinch OREGANO

Makes 1 serving.

FRUIT SALAD–Stir together in small bowl

2 tablespoons MAYONNAISE or SOUR CREAM
1 teaspoon ORANGE JUICE (or juice from any canned fruit you may use)
SUGAR, to taste
Gently toss with fruit

Makes 1 serving.

LEMON & OIL–Shake together in jar with tight-fitting lid

½ cup VEGETABLE OIL
⅓ cup LEMON JUICE
1 tablespoon SUGAR
dash SALT
1 teaspoon PAPRIKA

Makes enough salad dressing for several salads.

THREE SALAD DRESSINGS

3 Minutes

Salad
Dressings

Small Bowl or
Jar With Tight Lid

No Cooking

CHUTNEY SALAD DRESSING

2 Minutes
Serves 1

¼ cup SOUR CREAM or PLAIN YOGURT
2 tablespoons MANGO or PEACH CHUTNEY
¼ teaspoon SPICY-STYLE MUSTARD
juice of ¼ LEMON

Using measuring cup, stir together the sour cream and chutney. (You may have to cut up the fruit slightly in the chutney.)

Salad
Dressings

Measuring Cup
No Cooking

NEED:
    ½ cup VEGETABLE OIL
    ¼ cup WINE VINEGAR
    2 teaspoons SUGAR
    ¼ teaspoon SALT
    ¼ cup CATSUP

STEP 1:Dump all ingredients into jar with lid.
STEP 2:Shake to mix well.
STEP 3:Chill in refrigerator until ready to use. Keeps 1–2 weeks.

SWEET AND SOUR FRENCH DRESSING

5 Minutes
Makes 1 Cup

Salad
Dressings

Jar With Tight-Fitting Lid
No Cooking

Handy Hint

Made too many pancakes? Freeze the extras in a plastic bag with a sheet of waxed paper between layers. Remove from freezer number of pancakes needed and reheat in microwave on highest setting for 30 seconds.

❖

EZ clean for microwave oven: Set a bowl of hot water in microwave oven for 30 minutes. Dried food absorbs water and wipes off easily.

❖

When making sauces in microwave: Use cups twice the height of liquids to keep sauces from bubbling over.

MICROWAVE MAGIC

NEED:
  FLOUR TORTILLAS
  CHEDDAR CHEESE, sliced or shredded
  BUTTER or MARGARINE

OPTIONAL FILLINGS:
  SALSA, BARBECUE SAUCE, thin sliced HAM, thin sliced COOKED
  CHICKEN, mild CHILI PEPPERS, thin sliced ONIONS

STEP 1: Butter tortilla and lay on paper towel. Cover with cheese and top with whatever toppings appeal to you. Butter second tortilla and lay over fillings with butter side facing fillings.

STEP 2: Place quesadilla on paper towel and place in microwave. Microwave on HIGH 1½ to 2 minutes. Remove to plate and let cool a few minutes before cutting into triangles (pizza style).

Everyone's Favorite Quesadillas

3 Minutes
Serves 1

Microwave Magic

Paper Towel

FISH & BROCCOLI

5 Minutes
Serves 1

Microwave Magic

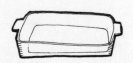

Microwave-Safe Shallow
Baking Dish

NEED:

1 large piece uncooked chunky FISH
2 stalks FROZEN BROCCOLI
tablespoon BUTTER or MARGARINE
splash WHITE WINE
Optional:
sprinkle of DILL WEED, THYME, or TARRAGON

STEP 1: Place fish in microwave-safe shallow baking dish. Top with broccoli stalks. Dot with butter. Sprinkle with herbs (if you have them). Spoon wine over all.

STEP 2: Cover tightly with plastic wrap. Cook on HIGH 5 minutes or till fish is flaky.

If you like it saucy, top with a couple spoonfuls of cheddar cheese soup (straight from the can). Do this during the final 2 minutes of cooking.

NEED:
    RUSSET or WHITE POTATOES
    VEGETABLE OIL

STEP 1: Wash and scrub potatoes to remove all dirt. Rub each potato with oil. Poke with fork in several places around potato.

STEP 2: Microwave on HIGH approximately 4 minutes per potato. Cooking time will vary depending on size, shape, and density of potato.

STEP 3: When potato feels soft to the touch, remove and wrap in a paper towel or cloth and let sit 5 minutes. Potato will stay hot at least 30 minutes. Cut open and fill as you want.

QUICK MASHED POTATOES

Scoop out inside of well-cooked potato and mash with fork, adding 1 tablespoon butter and 1 tablespoon of milk to make it creamier. Salt and pepper to taste.

POTATOES, BAKED OR MASHED

4 Minutes
Serves 1

Microwave Magic

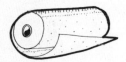

Paper Towel

Simply Basic Sauces

....

4 Minutes
Serves 1

Microwave Magic

Large Microwave-Safe Bowl

SOUPER SAUCE

Use can of condensed cream-style soup (not the ready-to-eat style). Empty soup into microwave-safe bowl and heat on HIGH 3 minutes.

NOTE: NEVER put metal cans in microwave ovens (metal will spark and ignite under microwaves).

BASIC WHITE CREAM SAUCE
NEED:
  2 tablespoons BUTTER or MARGARINE
  2 tablespoons FLOUR
  1 cup MILK
  dash SALT

STEP 1: In large bowl, melt butter or margarine in microwave on HIGH 30 seconds.
STEP 2: Remove bowl from microwave and gradually stir in flour till well blended. Then stir in milk and salt. (Mixture may be slightly lumpy, but lumps disappear when cooked.) Heat on HIGH 2 minutes.
STEP 3: Remove, then give final stir. Cook on HIGH 2 more minutes or till smooth and creamy.

Use the directions for Basic White Cream Sauce (see preceding page).
Follow Step 1 and Step 2, then:

CHEESE SAUCE

Before you start Step 3, stir in 2 handfuls shredded cheddar cheese. Continue
with directions for Step 3.

BASIL-TOMATO SAUCE

Before you start Step 3, stir in 1 teaspoon tomato sauce and ¼ teaspoon dried
basil (in spice section of market). Continue with directions for Step 3.

Try over spinach pasta.

MUSTARD SAUCE

Before you start Step 3, stir in 1 teaspoon spicy mustard. Continue with directions for Step 3.

Use with hot dogs as a dipping sauce.

LEMON SAUCE

Before you start Step 3, stir in 2 teaspoons lemon juice and 1 teaspoon butter or
margarine. Continue with Step 3.

Excellent over fish or vegetables.

SIMPLY BASIC SAUCES: VARIATIONS

4 Minutes
Serves 1

Large Microwave-Safe Bowl

SCRAMBLED EGGS PERFECTO

....

1 to 1½ Minutes
Serves 1

Microwave Magic

Glass Measuring Cup

NEED:
1 or 2 EGGS
SALT, PEPPER to taste

STEP 1: Crack egg(s) into a glass measuring cup. Beat well with a fork till all is yellow.
STEP 2: Cover cup tightly with plastic wrap.
STEP 3: Microwave at 70 percent, 1 minute for 1 egg (1½ minutes for 2 eggs). Should be perfect, but if you like your eggs done more, continue cooking at 70 percent, checking every 20 seconds.

Spoon out onto plate, add salt and pepper, and eat.

NEVER microwave eggs in their shells: They will EXPLODE!!

NEED:

    1 large ACORN SQUASH (it is the round dark-green one with ridges)
    scoop of COTTAGE CHEESE
    sprinkle WALNUTS, chopped
    1 tablespoon MARGARINE
    SALT, PEPPER to taste

STEP 1: Make about 6 small slits with a sharp knife around outside of squash. Only slit to inside center of squash; do not cut all the way through or cut open the squash.

STEP 2: Set in microwave. (No need for dish or paper towel under it.) Cook on HIGH 10 minutes.

NOTE: If you do not have a revolving base in your microwave, you will need to rotate the squash after the first 5 minutes, then continue cooking the remaining 5 minutes.

STEP 3: Remove the squash from microwave and let it sit about 5 to 10 minutes before cutting it open. (It is too hot to handle.) Then cut in half and remove seeds and pulp.

Fill squash with cottage cheese; top with walnuts. Add some butter and salt and pepper if you want.

10 Minutes
Serves 1–2

Microwave Magic

Sharp Knife

TEQUILA-SOAKED FISH

10 Minutes
Serves 1–2

Microwave Magic

Microwave-Safe Shallow
Baking Dish

NEED:
¼ cup BUTTER or MARGARINE
handful sliced ALMONDS
juice of 1 LEMON
sprinkle of DILL WEED (in spice section of market)
SALT, PEPPER to taste
1 tablespoon TEQUILA
1 or 2 pieces white CHUNKY FISH (bass, halibut, turbot, etc.)

STEP 1: Put butter and almonds in microwave-safe shallow baking dish. Cook on HIGH 3 minutes, stir, then continue on HIGH 2 more minutes or till almonds are golden. Remove from microwave oven.

STEP 2: Stir in rest of ingredients, laying fish on top. Spoon some of the sauce over fish.

STEP 3: Cover with plastic wrap. Cook on HIGH 5 minutes or till fish is flaky. (Don't overcook or fish will be tough.)

Serve this with packaged rice mix and spoon sauce over.

NEED:
    large-size FLOUR TORTILLAS
    HOT DOGS
    BUTTER or MARGARINE

OPTIONAL CONDIMENTS:
    BARBECUE SAUCE or CATSUP, CHILI, shredded CHEESE, MUSTARD,
    PICKLE RELISH

STEP 1: Butter tortilla and spread lightly with any condiment you like.
STEP 2: Lay hot dog on edge of tortilla and roll up. Wrap paper towel around
        tortilla dog.
STEP 3: Microwave on HIGH 1 to 2 minutes. Remove hot dog from
        microwave oven. Let hot dog remain wrapped up for one minute to
        cool before eating.

TORTILLA DOG

2 Minutes
Serves 1

Microwave Magic

Paper Towel

HANDY HINT

For fresh parsley and alfalfa sprouts, grow your own in small pots by a sunny window.

❖

Mushrooms will keep fresh up to a week if you wrap them *unwashed* in paper towels.

❖

Chopping garlic: If you lay the flat side of a broad knife on top of a garlic clove and give it a whack with the palm of your hand, the garlic skin will slip off easily.

Vegetarian Main Meals

ANGEL PASTA WITH OLIVE OIL & GARLIC

8 Minutes
Serves 1

NEED:
- ¼ pound ANGEL HAIR or VERMICELLI PASTA
- ¼ cup OLIVE OIL
- 3 cloves GARLIC, peeled and cut into tiny pieces or slivers
- SALT and PEPPER, to taste
- handful cut-up FRESH BASIL or FRESH PARSLEY LEAVES
- 1 medium TOMATO, chopped into small pieces

Cook pasta according to directions on package and drain well.
Don't overcook.

STEP 1: In skillet, heat oil on high heat. Add garlic, salt, and pepper. Stir and cook 4 minutes. Turn heat *off.*

STEP 2: Add hot cooked, and well-drained pasta to sauce in skillet and toss well.

STEP 3: Add tomato and basil or parsley and toss gently. Enjoy!

Just eat it right out of the pan. No one's looking!

Vegetarian Main Meals

Saucepan (for the pasta)

Skillet

Top of Stove

High Heat

Fresh Veggie "Cool Pizza"

15 Minutes
Serves 1–2

Vegetarian Main Meals

Cookie Sheet (or flat pan)
Small Bowl
375° Oven

NEED:
1 can refrigerated CRESCENT ROLLS
1 4-ounce carton softened CREAM CHEESE
spoonful MAYONNAISE
couple leaves of FRESH BASIL, cut up
3 cloves of GARLIC, cut into tiny pieces
assorted FRESH VEGETABLES cut into bite sizes: TOMATOES, MUSHROOMS, ONIONS, PEPPERS, BROCCOLI, etc.

Preheat oven to 375°.

STEP 1: On flat cookie sheet, spread out crescent rolls with edges touching. Bake for 8 minutes in 375° oven. Set aside to cool.
STEP 2: In small bowl, blend together cream cheese, mayonnaise, dill, basil, and garlic.
STEP 3: Spread over cooled "pizza crust." Top with fresh vegetables.

NEED:

- 1 cup MILK
- ½ cup PACKAGED PANCAKE MIX (e.g., Bisquick)
- 2 EGGS
- 2 tablespoons BUTTER or MARGARINE
- ¾ cup grated JACK, WHITE, CHEDDAR, or SWISS CHEESE
- ½ cup FROZEN CUT-UP BROCCOLI

Preheat oven to 350°.

STEP 1: Combine all ingredients, except broccoli, in blender container. Blend on low speed 1 minute.

STEP 2: Thaw broccoli in cold water, drain, and pat dry with paper towel.

STEP 3: Spread a bit of butter around inside of pie pan. Lay broccoli in bottom of pie pan. Pour blender mixture over broccoli (being careful not to spill over sides). Bake in 350° oven 40 minutes or till quiche is puffy and golden and doesn't jiggle when you move it.

You might want to try this with spinach for a terrific spinach quiche!!

QUICHE IN A BLENDER

45 Minutes
Serves 3–4

Vegetarian Main Meals

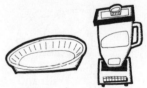

Blender &
8-Inch Pie Pan
350° Oven

Shepherd's Pie Tofu Style

15 Minutes
Serves 1–2

Vegetarian Main Meals

Skillet With Lid
Top of Stove
Medium High to
Medium Heat

NEED:

INSTANT MASHED POTATOES, prepared for 1 or 2 servings as directed on package
2 tablespoons OLIVE OIL
½ ONION, cut up
Couple handfuls sliced MUSHROOMS
4 ounces FIRM TOFU, cut into 1-inch cubes
squirt of SOY SAUCE
1 10-ounce package frozen MIXED VEGETABLES
SALT and PEPPER, to taste
couple handfuls shredded CHEDDAR CHEESE

STEP 1: In skillet, on medium high, heat olive oil 1 minute. Add onion, mushrooms, tofu, and soy sauce. Stir gently and cook until onion is limp and transparent, about 3 minutes.

STEP 2: Stir in frozen vegetables adding a couple shakes of salt and pepper. Cook 2–3 minutes or until vegetables are just barely tender.

STEP 3: Drop mounds of mashed potatoes over mixture.

STEP 4: Sprinkle with cheddar cheese. Cover with lid and cook on medium heat for 5 minutes or until cheese is melted and potatoes are steaming hot.

NEED:

    2 tablespoons VEGETABLE OIL
    1 ONION, chopped
    ½ GREEN BELL PEPPER, chopped
    1 5-ounce can TOMATO SAUCE
    1 can WATER (use empty tomato sauce can)
    spoonful SALSA
    dash SALT, PEPPER
    ½ cup RICE (uncooked)

STEP 1: Heat oil in skillet on high heat. Add onion and bell pepper. Stir and cook till onion is limp.

STEP 2: Stir in rest of ingredients. When mixture starts to boil, turn heat to lowest setting. Cover and cook about 18 minutes or till liquid is absorbed.

SPANISH RICE

....

20 Minutes
Serves 1–2

Vegetarian Main Meals

Skillet
Top of Stove
High to Lowest Heat

SURPRISE "MEAT" LOAF

....

1½ Hours
Serves 3–4

Vegetarian Main Meals

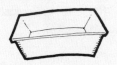

2-Quart Loaf Pan
350° Oven

NEED:

    2 cups BREAD CRUMBS (see below)
    1 cup WALNUTS, finely ground (see below)
    ½ cup MILK
    2 EGGS
    1 teaspoon GARLIC SALT
    1 teaspoon DRIED PARSLEY
    1 teaspoon SAGE (in spice section of market)

Preheat oven to 350°.

STEP 1: Thoroughly mix all ingredients together in a large mixing bowl.

STEP 2: Grease loaf-shaped baking dish generously with margarine. Pour mixture into dish.

STEP 3: Bake in 350° oven approximately 1½ hours or till knife inserted into loaf comes out dry. Remove from oven and let cool till you can remove easily onto plate. Tastes great hot or cold in sandwiches.

Use your blender to make quick bread crumbs. Simply tear a slice of bread into quarters and blend on medium speed until crumbly. Best to do 1 slice at a time. You will need 3 to 4 slices bread for 2 cups crumbs.

Need finely ground nuts? Use your blender again.

NEED:

    1 large BAKING POTATO (washed and scrubbed clean)
    1 10-ounce package frozen chopped BROCCOLI
    1 GREEN ONION, chopped (green ends included)
    dash SALT, BLACK PEPPER
    2 tablespoons softened CREAM CHEESE
    handful shredded CHEDDAR CHEESE

Preheat oven to 375°.

STEP 1: Cook broccoli according to directions on package.

STEP 2: Pierce skin on potato with fork 4–5 times, then bake potato. Either microwave potato, on high, *5 minutes,* OR bake *40 minutes* in 375° oven. Let cool until able to handle.

STEP 3: Slice long edge off top of potato to make a boat. Scoop out potato pulp and place in mixing bowl. Add cream cheese and mash with fork. Stir in onion, salt, pepper, and broccoli.

STEP 4: Spoon potato mixture back into skin. Sprinkle with cheese and set potato on sheet of foil in oven. Back 10 minutes or until cheese is hot and bubbly.

Too-Stuffed Potato

15–60 Minutes
(depending on method
of baking potato)
Serves 1

Vegetarian Main Meals

Small Pan
Mixing Bowl
Microwave or
375° Oven

VEGETABLES SUPREME

15 Minutes
Serves 1–2

Vegetarian Main Meals

Skillet
Top of Stove
High to Medium Heat

NEED:

3 tablespoons VEGETABLE OIL (or better yet, OLIVE OIL)
1 ZUCCHINI, thinly sliced
2 CARROTS, thinly sliced
½ each RED and GREEN BELL PEPPER, chopped into bite-size pieces
1 ONION, thinly sliced
(any other fresh veg you want, sliced thin)
½ small head RED CABBAGE (important ingredient)
1 tablespoon WINE VINEGAR
SALT, PEPPER to taste

STEP 1: In large skillet, on high heat, heat oil till hot (drop of water will sizzle in pan). Carefully add all vegetables except cabbage. Stir and fry about 5 minutes or till vegetables are bright in color and still crispy.

STEP 2: Add cabbage, vinegar, salt, and pepper. Stir and fry on medium heat 10 minutes or till all ingredients are hot and cabbage becomes tender and slightly limp.

Tastes wonderful with buttered pasta.

Zucchini & Eggs Frittata

....

15 Minutes
Serves 1–2

NEED:

2 tablespoons VEGETABLE OIL
½ small ONION, thinly sliced
1 small RED POTATO, thinly sliced
1 ZUCCHINI, thinly sliced
splash SOY SAUCE
sprinkle PARMESAN CHEESE
4 EGGS, lightly beaten with fork

STEP 1: In skillet, on high heat, cook onions and potato in hot oil till onion is transparent (approximately 2 minutes).

STEP 2: Add zucchini, soy sauce, and Parmesan cheese. Reduce heat to medium low. Cook 5 minutes, stirring occasionally.

STEP 3: Pour eggs over vegetables. Cover and cook on low heat 5 minutes. Eggs will puff like an omelet.

Vegetarian Main Meals

Skillet With Lid
Top of Stove
High to Low Heat

Handy Hint

Safety tip: Always wash counter surface with hot soapy water and rinse well both before and after preparing poultry. This helps to prevent salmonella bacteria from forming or being transferred to other foods.

❖

Recrisp "soggy" refrigerated fried chicken, uncovered in a hot 400° oven.

❖

Remove the skin from turkey or chicken before or after cooking and reduce the fat by almost half.

CHICKEN & TURKEY

....

45 Minutes
Serves 1–2

NEED:
2 skinless and boneless CHICKEN BREASTS or THIGHS
couple sprinkles of LAWRY'S SEASONED SALT
dash BLACK PEPPER
1 15-ounce can SAUERKRAUT, drained
4 slices SWISS CHEESE
½ cup THOUSAND ISLAND SALAD DRESSING

Preheat oven to 350°.

STEP 1: Prepare baking dish: Rub bottom of dish with a dab of margarine, butter or vegetable oil, or use nonstick cooking spray to prevent chicken from sticking.

STEP 2: Lay chicken in bottom of baking dish. Sprinkle with seasoned salt and black pepper.

STEP 3: Spoon sauerkraut and Thousand Island salad dressing over chicken and top with Swiss cheese.

STEP 4: Cover dish with aluminum foil. Bake at 350° for 40 minutes.

Chicken & Turkey

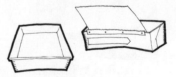

Oven Baking Dish
Aluminum Foil
350° Oven

CHICKEN IN MUSHROOM SAUCE

25 Minutes
Serves 1–2

Chicken & Turkey

Skillet With Lid

Small Bowl

Top of Stove

Medium High to Low Heat

NEED:

2 tablespoons BUTTER or MARGARINE
couple handfuls sliced MUSHROOMS
¼ ONION, chopped
3–4 boneless and skinless CHICKEN THIGHS
couple shakes LAWRY'S SEASONED SALT
1 10-ounce can CREAM OF MUSHROOM SOUP
¼ cup MILK
splash WHITE WINE

STEP 1: In skillet, on medium high heat, melt butter. Add onion and mushrooms. Stir and cook 2 minutes or until onion is limp.

STEP 2: Rinse chicken thighs and pat dry with paper towels. Add chicken to skillet and sprinkle with seasoned salt. Cook chicken, turning to lightly brown on both sides.

STEP 3: In small bowl, mix together mushroom soup, milk, and wine. Pour over chicken. When soup mixture starts to boil turn heat to lowest setting.

STEP 4: Cover and cook 20 minutes.

Try tossing in a couple handfuls frozen peas during the last few minutes of cooking. Then serve over hot fettuccine or buttered noodles.

NEED:
1 FRYING CHICKEN, cut up
SALT, PEPPER to taste
1 can DIET ORANGE SODA
¼ cup SOY SAUCE

Preheat oven to 325°.

STEP 1: Wash chicken (remove skin) and pat dry with paper towels. Salt and pepper chicken and place in foil-lined broiler pan.
STEP 2: Mix together orange soda and soy sauce. Pour over chicken.
STEP 3: Bake in 325° oven 1 hour or till chicken is tender. Spoon sauce over chicken a couple of times while cooking.

Great to nibble on the next day.

CHICKEN ON A DIET

1 Hour
Serves 3–4

Chicken & Turkey

Foil-Lined Broiler Pan
325° Oven

CURRIED CHICKEN

50 Minutes
Serves 1–2

Chicken & Turkey

Pie Pan &
Foil-Lined Broiler Pan
350° Oven

NEED:
3–4 CHICKEN PARTS
¼ cup HONEY
2 teaspoons MUSTARD
2 tablespoons SOY SAUCE
½ teaspoon CURRY POWDER (spice section of market)

Preheat oven to 350°.

STEP 1: Mix together in pie pan to make sauce: honey, mustard, soy sauce, curry powder.

STEP 2: Wash chicken and pat dry with paper toweling. Dip chicken in sauce to coat well. Place on foil-lined broiler pan.

STEP 3: Bake uncovered in 350° oven 30 minutes. Turn chicken pieces over and bake 20–30 more minutes or till chicken is tender.

Stick a potato in oven to bake as chicken cooks.

NEED:

1 TURKEY LEG or BREAST
¼ cup MARGARINE or BUTTER, melted
SALT, BLACK PEPPER, PAPRIKA, GARLIC SALT
1 teaspoon POULTRY SEASONING

Preheat oven to 350°.

STEP 1: Wash turkey and pat dry with paper towel.
STEP 2: Pour melted butter into foil-lined baking pan. Lay turkey in pan, turning to coat all over with butter.
STEP 3: Sprinkle with seasonings. Cover pan with foil and bake in 350° oven 40 minutes.
STEP 4: Remove foil and spoon buttery juices over turkey. Bake uncovered 40–50 minutes, basting every 15 minutes with buttery juices until turkey is tender and starts to fall away from bone.

Add some hot *mashed potatoes and turkey gravy.*
And top off with cranberry sauce!

1½–2 Hours
Serves 1

Chicken & Turkey

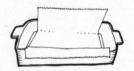

Foil-Lined Baking Dish
350° Oven

73

Gizzards in Gravy

60 Minutes
Several Servings

Chicken & Turkey

Saucepan With Lid
Top of Stove
High to Low Heat

NEED:

1 package uncooked CHICKEN GIZZARDS
2 cups WATER
½ ONION, chopped
½ teaspoon INSTANT CHICKEN BOUILLON
SALT, PEPPER to taste
⅓ cup FLOUR
¼ cup WATER

STEP 1: Wash chicken and place in saucepan. Add 2 cups water, onion, bouillon, dash each salt and pepper. Bring to boil on high heat.

STEP 2: Reduce heat to very low. Cover and cook slowly 1 hour.

STEP 3: In separate cup, stir flour into water till smooth. Slowly pour into chicken and broth, stirring constantly. Turn heat up to medium. Cook and stir 2 minutes.

Serve over hot rice or noodles.

....

1 Hour
Serves 1–2

NEED:
3–4 CHICKEN PIECES
½ cup bottled BARBECUE SAUCE
2 tablespoons MARGARINE, melted
large tablespoon BROWN SUGAR
SALT, PEPPER

Preheat oven to 350°.

STEP 1: Wash chicken and pat dry with paper towels. In small bowl, stir together barbecue sauce, margarine, and brown sugar.

STEP 2: Lay chicken in foil-lined broiler pan. Season with salt and pepper. Brush half of sauce mixture on chicken and bake uncovered in 350° oven 30 minutes.

STEP 3: Turn chicken pieces over and brush with rest of sauce. Cook till tender, 20 or 30 more minutes.

Chicken & Turkey

If there is too much liquid in pan, spoon some out.

Foil-Lined Broiler Pan
350° Oven

SAUSAGES & MASH

30 Minutes
Serves 1–2

Chicken & Turkey

Skillet
Top of Stove
High to Medium Heat

FIRST: *Make Mom's Mashed Potatoes (page 120) or make 1 serving of instant mashed potatoes as directed on package.*

NEED:
  4 CHICKEN or TURKEY SAUSAGES (not precooked), pierced a few times with fork
  ½ GREEN BELL PEPPER, cut into strips
  ½ ONION, cut into strips
  ¼ cup bottled STEAK SAUCE (e.g., Heinz 57, A-1, or HP Sauce)

STEP 1: Lay sausages in skillet with just enough water to barely cover them. Turn heat to high. When water starts to boil, turn heat to medium and gently cook 15 minutes. (Check to make sure water doesn't boil out of pan.) Drain off any excess water.

STEP 2: Add bell pepper and onion and cook on medium heat until vegetables are done to your liking, about 5 minutes.

STEP 3: Stir in steak sauce. Cover and cook 5 minutes.

STEP 4: Serve over the hot mashed potatoes.

NEED:
- 4 DRUMSTICKS or 2 whole CHICKEN LEGS (and THIGHS)
- 2 tablespoons MAYONNAISE
- 1 cup crushed CORN CHIPS
- 1 teaspoon CHILI POWDER
- dash SALT
- teaspoon MARGARINE

Preheat oven to 375°.

STEP 1: Wash chicken and pat dry with paper towels. Spread mayonnaise on chicken.

STEP 2: In small bowl, combine corn chips, chili powder, and salt. Stir well. Roll chicken in mixture.

STEP 3: Generously grease pan with margarine. Lay chicken in pan. Bake in 375° oven 40 minutes or till chicken is browned and tender.

To tell if chicken is cooked: The juices of cooked chicken will run clear (not pink) when pierced with a fork.

40 Minutes
Serves 1–2

Chicken & Turkey

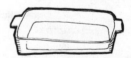

Shallow Baking Dish
375° Oven

Turkey Dogs & Pepper Strips

15 Minutes
Serves 1

Chicken & Turkey

Skillet With Lid
Top of Stove
High to Medium Low Heat

NEED:

1 tablespoon VEGETABLE OIL
½ ONION, sliced
1 clove GARLIC, sliced into very thin pieces
½ GREEN BELL PEPPER, cut into thin strips
4 TURKEY HOT DOGS, cut lengthwise in quarters
juice of ½ LEMON
splash SOY SAUCE

STEP 1: In skillet, on high heat, heat oil. Add onion, garlic, and bell pepper strips. Cook until onion is limp.

STEP 2: Add turkey frank strips. Stir and cook 5 minutes or until meat and vegetables are lightly browned.

STEP 3: Add lemon juice and soy sauce, and stir slightly. Turn heat to medium low. Cover and cook 5 minutes.

Serve this yummy meal over toasted hamburger buns.

NEED:

  1 tablespoon VEGETABLE or OLIVE OIL
  ¼ ONION, chopped
  dash GARLIC SALT
  ¾ pound GROUND TURKEY
  1 11-ounce can MEXI-CORN, *not drained*
  1 10-ounce can CREAM OF TOMATO SOUP
  SALT and PEPPPER to taste

STEP 1: In skillet, on high heat, heat oil and add onion, garlic, and ground
        turkey. Stir and cook until meat is no longer pink in color. Drain off
        any excess liquid.
STEP 2: Add and stir in tomato soup, corn, salt, and black pepper. Cover pan.
        Turn heat to medium and cook 5 minutes.

30 Minutes
Serves 2

Chicken & Turkey

Skillet With Lid
Top of Stove
High to Medium Heat

Other Chicken & Turkey Recipes Found in This Cookbook

HANDY HINT

When a recipe calls for bread crumb toppings, try using ready-to-eat
flaked cereal instead.

FISH & SHELLFISH

NEED:

1 small can TUNA, drained
½ cup SOUR CREAM
2 GREEN ONIONS, sliced
handful BLACK OLIVES, sliced or cut in halves
4 FLOUR TORTILLAS
1 cup shredded CHEDDAR CHEESE
GREEN CHILI SALSA (in ethnic food section of market)

STEP 1: In small bowl, mix together tuna, just *2 tablespoons* of the sour cream, green onions, and olives.
STEP 2: Lay tortillas flat. In center of tortilla, spread ¼ of the tuna mixture, sprinkle with a handful of cheese. Fold in ends of tortillas, then roll up and lay in baking dish.
STEP 3: Repeat with rest of tortillas.
STEP 4: Sprinkle with any remaining cheese. Cover and bake at 325° for 20 minutes.

Serve topped with a plop of remaining sour cream and a spoonful of green chili salsa.

BAKED TUNA QUESADILLAS

20 Minutes
Serves 1–2

Fish & Shellfish

Baking Dish
(rub dish with vegetable oil
or dab of margarine to
prevent sticking)
325° Oven

CLAM SLAW GREEK STYLE

5 Minutes
Serves 1–2

Fish &
Shellfish

Large Bowl
No Cooking

NEED:
½ bag preshredded CABBAGE SLAW MIX
1 4-ounce can chopped BLACK OLIVES, drained
handful WALNUTS, chopped
1 6½-ounce can minced CLAMS, well drained
couple spoonfuls RAISINS
SALT, PEPPER to taste
1 cup MAYONNAISE
1 tablespoon VINEGAR (wine vinegar is best)

STEP 1: Dump cabbage, olives, nuts, clams, and raisins into large bowl.
STEP 2: In small bowl or cup, blend mayonnaise and vinegar together. Pour over slaw mixture. Season to taste and serve.

Use as a filling for pita bread, or eat right out of the bowl.

NEED:
2 FROZEN FISH STICKS, the chunky kind
4 CORN TORTILLAS (soft uncooked)
handful shredded CABBAGE
½ TOMATO, chopped
spoonful bottled TARTAR SAUCE
sprinkle shredded CHEDDAR CHEESE
large spoonful SALSA

STEP 1: Cook fish according to directions on package.
STEP 2: Heat skillet on high heat 1 minute. Lay tortilla in skillet and heat on one side for a few seconds; turn over and heat other side. When tortilla is hot and limp, remove and continue with second tortilla.
STEP 3: Place two hot tortillas together and lay hot cooked fish in center. Sprinkle with cabbage, cheese, tomato, tartar sauce, and salsa. Fold in half and eat "taco style."

The recipe makes two tacos. If you want more, make sure you use two tortillas for each fish taco.

FISH TACOS

10 Minutes
Serves 1

Fish & Shellfish

Skillet
Top of Stove
High Heat

Poached Fish in Foil

20 Minutes
Serves 1

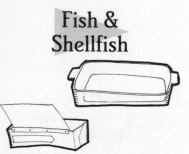

**Fish &
Shellfish**

Heavy Duty Aluminum Foil
Broiler Pan or Baking Dish
350° Oven

NEED:

    1 single serving size piece FRESH FISH (chunky or thick fillet)
    juice of ½ LEMON
    1 CARROT, sliced thinly
    1 GREEN ONION, sliced thinly
    1 TOMATO, chopped
    1 sprig of PARSLEY, cut up
    several pats of BUTTER or MARGARINE

Preheat oven to 350°.

STEP 1: Place fish in center of foil.

STEP 2: Sprinkle vegetables, lemon juice, butter, and parsley over fish.

STEP 3: Wrap tightly in foil and set in baking dish. Bake 15–20 minutes, depending on the thickness of fish.

Fish cooks quickly. *Don't ruin fresh fish by overcooking.*
Fish should be light and flaky when pierced with a fork.

NEED:
1 EGG
1 6-ounce can SALMON, not drained
1 GREEN ONION, sliced thinly
12 RITZ or SALTINE CRACKERS, crushed to crumbs
2 tablespoons VEGETABLE OIL

STEP 1: In small bowl, combine egg, salmon with liquid in can, green onion, and ½ cracker crumbs. Mix well.
STEP 2: Using your hands, shape the mixture into 3 balls and flatten into patties.
STEP 3: Dump remaining crumbs into pie pan or shallow dish. Coat both sides of salmon patties with crumbs.
STEP 4: In skillet, on high heat, heat oil 1 minute or until very hot. Lay patties carefully in skillet. Cook each side 3 to 4 minutes or until browned on each side.

SALMON PATTIES

15 Minutes
Serves 1

Fish & Shellfish

Small Bowl

Pie Plate or Shallow Dish

Skillet

Top of Stove, High Heat

Shellfish Au Gratin

30 Minutes
Serves 2

Fish & Shellfish

Baking Dish

Small Saucepan

Top of Stove

375° Oven

NEED:

¼ pound SCALLOPS or SHRIMP
1 8-ounce can GREEN BEANS, drained
1 cup MILK
2 tablespoons FLOUR
2 tablespoons BUTTER or MARGARINE
dash SALT
½ cup SWISS CHEESE, shredded
handful CRACKER CRUMBS
1 tablespoon BUTTER or MARGARINE

Preheat oven to 375°.

STEP 1: Lay green beans over bottom of baking dish. Lay scallops or shrimp on top of broccoli. Set aside.
STEP 2: In small saucepan, stir together milk, flour, butter, and salt. Turn heat to medium. Cook and stir until sauce is hot and starts to bubble. (Sauce should be thick and creamy.)
STEP 3: Turn *heat off* and stir in Swiss cheese until cheese is melted.
STEP 4: Pour sauce over shellfish and green beans. Sprinkle with crumbs and dot with bits of butter or margarine. Bake in 375° oven 20 minutes or until sauce is bubbly.

NEED:
  4 EGGS
  dash BLACK PEPPER
  4 MUSHROOMS, washed and chopped small
  handful WATER CHESTNUTS, chopped small
  1 stalk CELERY, chopped small
  handful fresh BEAN SPROUTS
  handful small precooked SHRIMP
  splash SOY SAUCE
  1 tablespoon VEGETABLE OIL

STEP 1: In large bowl, beat eggs using a fork. Add dash of black pepper. Stir in vegetables, shrimp, and soy sauce.

STEP 2: Heat oil in skillet on medium high heat. Soon mixture about the size of a pancake onto hot skillet. Cook until underside is browned.

STEP 3: Turn over and cook until eggs are set. Don't overcook or shrimp will be tough.

SHRIMP EGG FOO YUNG

8 Minutes
Serves 1–2

Fish & Shellfish

Large Bowl

Skillet

Top of Stove

Medium High Heat

91

SOMETHING DIFFERENT TUNA SALAD

5 Minutes
Serves 1–2

Fish &
Shellfish

Large Bowl

No Cooking

NEED:
1 6-ounce can TUNA, well drained
1 4-ounce can chopped BLACK OLIVES
2 GREEN ONIONS, thinly sliced
2 HARD-COOKED EGGS, chopped
¾ cup MAYONNAISE
1 teaspoon VINEGAR
SEASONED SALT
3 ounces CHOW MEIN NOODLES (optional)

Mix all together in bowl (except chow mein noodles). When ready to eat, top with chow mein noodles.

EXTRAS TO ADD:
1 stalk CELERY, chopped
1 CARROT, grated
1 2-ounce jar chopped PIMIENTOS
crumbled cooked BACON

chopped RED APPLES
spoonful sliced ALMONDS
spoonful SUNFLOWER SEEDS
handful BEAN SPROUTS
spoonful RAISINS

Filling enough for a whole meal!

Tuna Soufflé

45 Minutes
Serves 1–2

NEED:
- 4 slices BREAD (good way to use up stale bread)
- 4 slices CHEESE
- 6½-ounce can TUNA, drained
- 3 EGGS, beaten with fork till fluffy and yellow
- 1 cup MILK
- 1 GREEN ONION, sliced
- 1 2-ounce can SLICED MUSHROOMS
- dash SALT, PEPPER

STEP 1: Grease bottom and sides of baking dish with dab of margarine or vegetable oil. Lay 2 bread slices over bottom of baking dish. Top with cheese, tuna, and remaining 2 bread slices.

STEP 2: In small bowl, stir together eggs, milk, onion, mushrooms, salt, and pepper. Pour over layered mixture in baking dish. Set dish to the side for 15 minutes while you preheat oven to 350°.

STEP 3: Bake in 350° oven 45 minutes. Serve hot and puffy.

Fish & Shellfish

Shallow Baking Dish
350° Oven

HANDY HINT

Don't dump grease from cooked meat down drain!
Drain grease into old can and discard when solidified.

❖

To keep thin steaks or chops from curling when frying, clip the fatty edges
with kitchen knife every couple of inches.

❖

Cook ground meat within two days of buying to be sure of freshness.

MEATY MEALS

NEED:

    1 ONION, sliced thin
    1 clove GARLIC, mashed
    1 tablespoon MARGARINE
    ½ pound GROUND BEEF
    1 8-ounce can TOMATO SAUCE
    1 8-ounce can WHOLE KERNEL CORN
    splash HOT TACO SAUCE
    SALT, PEPPER to taste

STEP 1: In skillet, on medium heat, cook onion and garlic in margarine till golden.

STEP 2: Add ground beef. Stir and cook till beef loses pink color.

STEP 3: Stir in tomato sauce, corn, taco sauce, and seasonings. Reduce heat to lowest heat. Cover and cook 10 minutes.

Crunch up tortilla chips and sprinkle on top just before eating.

BEEF MEXICANA

15 Minutes
Serves 1–2

Meaty Meals

Skillet With Lid
Top of Stove
Medium to Lowest Heat

Best Beef Stew

4 Hours
Serves 2–3

Meaty
Meals

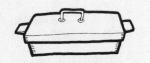

Ovenproof Pan With Lid
300 ° Oven (or slow cooker)

NEED:
1 pound lean STEWING BEEF
2 CARROTS, cut in chunks
2 ONIONS, cut in chunks
1 POTATO, cut in chunks
1 stalk CELERY, cut in chunks
1 15-ounce can cut-up TOMATOES, undrained
¼ cup MINUTE TAPIOCA (important ingredient)
dash of THYME and OREGANO
½ teaspoon SALT
1 heaping teaspoon INSTANT COFFEE
1 BEEF BOUILLON CUBE (or 1 teaspoon instant bouillon)
2 cups WATER

STEP 1: Dump all ingredients into a large ovenproof pan. Stir to mix well and cover.
STEP 2: Cook in 300° oven 4 hours or till meat is tender. (If you get the chance, stir a couple of times during cooking.)

If you use a slow cooker, you'll love the aroma when you come home starving after being in classes all day.

NEED:
- ½ pound GROUND BEEF
- ½ pound GROUND PORK SAUSAGE
- 1 EGG
- 12 SALTINE CRACKERS, smashed into crumbs
- 1 tablespoon MILK
- 1 10-ounce can CREAM OF MUSHROOM SOUP
- ½ empty soup can of BEER
- ½ thinly sliced ONION

STEP 1: In large bowl, mix together ground meat, egg, crumbs, and milk.

STEP 2: Shape into large ice-cream-scoop-sized balls.

STEP 3: Lay meatballs in skillet and set heat on high. Cook, turning meatballs until browned on all sides.

STEP 4: Add soup, water, beer, and onions. Cover pan. Turn heat to medium low and cook slowly 30 minutes or until meatballs are fully cooked.

Big Balls

....

40 Minutes
Serves 1–2

Meaty Meals

Large Mixing Bowl

Skillet

Top of Stove

High to Medium Low Heat

BISCUITS AND SAUSAGE GRAVY

....

20 Minutes
Serves 1–2

Meaty Meals

Baking Pan or Cookie Sheet

Skillet

Oven

Top of Stove

High to Medium Low Heat

NEED:
> 1 package refrigerated BISCUITS (baked according to directions)
> ½ pound GROUND PORK SAUSAGE
> 1 tablespoon MARGARINE (or leftover bacon grease, if you happen to have saved some)
> 2 tablespoons FLOUR
> 2 cups MILK
> SALT and PEPPER, to taste

Preheat oven and bake biscuits according to directions on package.

*While biscuits are baking—make **SAUSAGE GRAVY:***

STEP 1: Break up sausage an add to skillet. Turn heat to high. Stir and cook sausage until browned and crumbly, about 8 minutes. Drain off liquid.

STEP 2: Reduce heat to medium. Add margarine or bacon grease to sausage and stir to blend.

STEP 3: Add flour, stirring to mix well.

STEP 4: Turn heat to medium low. Add milk slowly, stirring continuously until mixture is thickened to the way you like gravy. Add salt and pepper to taste.

NEED:
4 wafer-thin PORK CHOPS
Couple dashes each of SALT, BLACK PEPPER, and PAPRIKA

Preheat broiler.

STEP 1: Sprinkle pork chops with seasonings on both sides of meat and set chops on rack of broiler pan.

STEP 2: Set under hot broiler and cook 5 minutes on one side.

STEP 3: Turn and broil 5 minutes on other side or until lightly browned.

Remember, pork should be white, not pink, when cut, but don't overcook as wafer-thin pork chops cook quickly.

10 Minutes
Serves 1

Meaty Meals

Broiler Pan
Oven Set at "Broil"

CHEAP ROAST

3 Hours
Serves 2–3

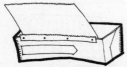

Heavy-Duty Aluminum Foil
350° Oven

NEED:

"Cheap" ROUND BONE or BLADE-CUT ROAST
1 package DRY ONION SOUP MIX
1 can condensed CREAM OF MUSHROOM SOUP
ALUMINUM FOIL, wide heavy-duty

Preheat oven to 350°.

STEP 1: Tear off about 2½–3 feet of foil. Fold in half.
STEP 2: Lay roast in middle of foil. Spread both soups over roast. Wrap and seal so juices won't drip out.
STEP 3: Cook in 350° oven 3 hours. Be careful when you unwrap foil, so juices won't spill.

No cleanup!

Makes its own gravy. Serve with mashed potatoes and a hot vegetable.

NEED:

   1 tablespoon VEGETABLE OIL
   ½ pound GROUND BEEF
   1 ONION, chopped
   1 clove GARLIC, minced
   ¼ GREEN BELL PEPPER, chopped
   1 can (15-ounce) CHILI
   1 can (15-ounce) KIDNEY BEANS
   1 15-ounce can CRUSHED TOMATOES (don't use stewed tomatoes)
   1-ounce jar SALSA (mild or hot, as you like it)
   ½ cup cheap RED WINE
   SALT, PEPPER

45 Minutes to 3 Hours
Serves 2–3

STEP 1: Heat oil in large saucepan on high heat. Add ground beef, onion and garlic. Stir and cook till meat is crumbly and browned. (Drain off excess grease into an old can to discard later.)

STEP 2: Add rest of ingredients and stir well. When chili starts to boil turn heat to lowest setting. Cover pan and cook slowly for at least ½ hour. Be sure to stir a couple of times during cooking.

If you have the time, cooking for 2 to 3 hours allows flavors to blend for an even better taste.

Meaty Meals

Large Saucepan With Lid
Top of Stove
High to Low Heat

Fast & Easy Meatballs

15 Minutes
15–20 Meatballs

Meaty Meals

Cookie Sheet or Broiler Pan
(without broiler rack)
350° Oven

NEED:

1 pound GROUND BEEF
⅔ cup packaged BREAD STUFFING MIX
2 teaspoons dry MINCED ONIONS (in spice section of market)
1 EGG
¾ cup WATER
1 teaspoon SALT
dash PEPPER

Preheat oven to 350°.

STEP 1: Dump all ingredients into large bowl; mix well. Shape into small balls (approximately 1½ inches).

STEP 2: Place on a cookie sheet or broiler pan and bake in 350° oven 15 minutes or till browned.

Use in spaghetti sauce, soups, and with gravies. Or slice and use in sandwiches. Freeze extra meatballs in plastic bag.

NEED:

2 tablespoons VEGETABLE OIL
½ pound STEWING BEEF, cut into ½-inch pieces, discard fatty part
¼ ONION, chopped
2 cloves GARLIC, cut into small pieces
10 BABY CARROTS
2 POTATOES, peeled and cut into chunks
couple dashes each PAPRIKA, GARLIC SALT, and PEPPER
pinch CRUSHED RED PEPPER (in spice section of market)
2 cups WATER
¼ cup RED WINE (optional, but good)

STEP 1: In heavy skillet, heat oil on high heat. Dump in meat and cook until browned on all sides.

STEP 2: Add vegetables, water, and spices. Bring to a boil. Turn heat to medium low. Cover and cook 1 hour.

STEP 3: Add wine and stir lightly. Cover and continue to cook 45–50 minutes or until meat is tender.

Serve over cooked noodles, top with a plop of sour cream and some sliced pickled beets (in canned vegetables section of supermarket)

2 Hours
Serves 1–2

Meaty Meals

Heavy Skillet
Top of Stove
High to Medium Low Heat

HUNGRY DAVE'S BEEF & BEANS

20 Minutes
Serves 1–2

Meaty Meals

Ovenproof Skillet

Top of Stove

High Heat

400° Oven

NEED:
½ pound GROUND BEEF
dash each SALT and PEPPER
1 10-ounce can PORK & BEANS
plop BARBECUE SAUCE
spoonful BROWN SUGAR
1 package REFRIGERATED BISCUITS
couple handfuls shredded CHEDDAR CHEESE
1 GREEN ONION, sliced

Preheat oven to 400°.

STEP 1: In skillet, on high heat, add ground beef. Stir and cook until meat is crumbly and brown. (Drain off excess grease into an old can.)

STEP 2: Stir in beans, barbecue sauce, brown sugar, salt, and pepper. Heat until bubbly.

STEP 3: Cut biscuits into quarters and cover beef mixture.

STEP 4: Sprinkle with cheese and heat in oven 15 minutes or until biscuits are browned.

A hearty meal for quick nourishment. Just add a green salad.

NEED:

　1 EGG
　¼ cup MILK
　2 slices SOFT BREAD, crumbled up
　1 pound GROUND BEEF
　1 4-ounce can MUSHROOMS (stems and pieces)
　couple plops CATSUP
　½ package DRY ONION SOUP MIX (shake well before using)

45 Minutes
Serves 2–3

Preheat oven to 350°.

STEP 1: In large bowl, beat egg with fork. Add milk and bread crumbs. Stir to mix.

STEP 2: Dump in rest of the ingredients and stir to mix well.

STEP 3: Dump mixture into oven baking dish and mold into a loaf. Bake in 350° oven 45 minutes or till done to your liking.

Makes great cold sandwiches next day.

Meaty Meals

Large Bowl
Baking Dish
350° Oven

Sausage, Kraut & Applesauce

15 Minutes
Serves 1–2

Meaty Meals

Skillet With Lid
Top of Stove
Medium Heat

NEED:
1 large fully cooked POLISH SAUSAGE
1 8-ounce can SAUERKRAUT
couple spoonfuls APPLESAUCE
spoonful BROWN SUGAR

STEP 1: Place sausage in skillet.
STEP 2: Add sauerkraut, applesauce, and brown sugar. Stir to mix.
STEP 3: Cover and cook on medium heat till hot (approximately 10–15 minutes).

Goes well with boiled potatoes and a green salad.

NEED:

1 tablespoon VEGETABLE OIL
½ pound GROUND BEEF
1 POTATO, cut in bite-size pieces
½ ONION, sliced thin
1 10-ounce can BEEF GRAVY
couple pinches PARSLEY (fresh, if available)
pinch of THYME (optional)
SALT, PEPPER to taste

STEP 1: In skillet, on medium heat, heat oil till hot. Add ground beef. Stir and cook till brown and crumbly. (Drain off excess fat into an old can.)

STEP 2: Add remaining ingredients; stir to mix.

STEP 3: Cover and cook on lowest heat 20 minutes, stirring occasionally.

In place of potato, use cooked noodles and reduce time in Step 3 to 10 minutes.

SLOP

25 Minutes
Serves 1–2

Meaty Meals

Skillet With Lid
Top of Stove
Medium to Low Heat

TAMALE & CHEESE DINNER

5 Minutes
Serves 1–2

Meaty
Meals

Skillet With Lid
Top of Stove
Low Heat

NEED:
1 can TAMALES
1 8-ounce can CORN, drained
handful grated CHEDDAR CHEESE

STEP 1: Unwrap tamales and break into pieces. Lay in skillet.
STEP 2: Top tamales with corn and sprinkle with cheese.
STEP 3: Cover with lid and cook on low heat 5 minutes or till hot.

Top with sliced avocado and spoonful cottage cheese or sour cream.

NEED:

    1 clove GARLIC, mashed
    1 small ONION, chopped
    ½ pound GROUND BEEF
    1 tablespoon VEGETABLE OIL
    1 16-ounce can WHOLE ITALIAN TOMATOES, cut up
    1 15-ounce can TOMATO SAUCE
    1 6-ounce can TOMATO PASTE
    splash BURGUNDY WINE
    1 teaspoon SALT
    1 tablespoon ITALIAN HERB SEASONING

STEP 1: In large saucepan, on medium heat, brown garlic and onion in hot oil. Add ground beef. Stir and cook till crumbly and browned. (Drain off grease into an old can, not down drain.)

STEP 2: Stir in rest of ingredients. When mixture comes to a boil, turn heat down to lowest setting. Cover tightly.

STEP 3: Cook slowly at least 1 hour. (Longer cooking enhances flavor.) Stir occasionally.

Serve over hot pasta.

THAT'S ITALIAN SPAGHETTI SAUCE

1¼ Hours (or longer)

Meaty Meals

Saucepan With Lid
Top of Stove
Medium to Lowest Heat

Handy Hint

Don't use too much salt when cooking:
You can always add more, but once it is in, you can't take it back.

❖

Garlic equations: 1 clove garlic equals ½ teaspoon finely chopped garlic equals ⅛ teaspoon garlic powder or dried minced garlic.

SIMPLY VEGGIES

BROILED POTATO SLICES

....

10 Minutes
Several Servings

NEED:

1 medium POTATO, washed (leave skin on)
VEGETABLE OIL
handful shredded CHEDDAR CHEESE

STEP 1: Slice potato into ¼-inch slices.
STEP 2: Lay slices on broiler pan rack. Brush each slice lightly with oil.
STEP 3: Broil till brown. Turn potatoes over, brush with oil and broil till brown. Sprinkle with cheese and broil a few more minutes till cheese melts.

Top with sour cream, bacon bits, and chives. Makes a great snack.

Simply
Veggies

Broiler Pan & Rack
Broil (highest heat in oven)

CARROT & POTATO PANCAKES

....

15 Minutes
Serves 1

Simply Veggies

Large Bowl

Skillet

Top of Stove

High Heat

NEED:
   1 large CARROT, peeled and shredded
   1 POTATO, peeled and shredded
   ¼ ONION, shredded
   BLACK PEPPER
   couple shakes LAWRY'S SEASONED SALT
   2 tablespoons VEGETABLE OIL

STEP 1: In large bowl, mix together shredded potato, carrot, and onion. Add seasonings.

STEP 2: In skillet, on high heat, heat oil 1 minute. Dump the carrot and potato mixture into skillet and press to form a large pancake.

STEP 3: Cook until pancake is browned on each side.

Tastes great with Broiled Wafer-Thin Pork Chops (page 101) and topped with store-bought cinnamon applesauce.

NEED:

  1 bunch SPINACH
  ¼ LEMON
  1 tablespoon MARGARINE
  SALT, PEPPER to taste

STEP 1: Wash spinach. *The easy way*: fill sink with water and dump loose spinach in. Break off stems at root, holding under water. (Both spinach leaves and stems are tasty.)

STEP 2: Shake off excess water and stuff spinach into saucepan. Add couple spoonfuls of water. Cover and cook at medium low heat 5 to 10 minutes or till tender.

STEP 3: Drain spinach and squeeze lemon on. Add margarine, salt, and pepper to taste.

Use a whole bunch—it shrinks a lot when cooked.

COOKED FRESH SPINACH

10 Minutes
Serves 1–2

Simply
Veggies

Saucepan With Lid
Top of Stove
Medium Low Heat

CORN ON THE COB

5 Minutes
Serves 1

Simply
Veggies

Large Saucepan With Lid
Top of Stove
High Heat

NEED:
1–2 ears fresh CORN ON COB
pat BUTTER or MARGARINE
SALT, PEPPER to taste

STEP 1: Tear off and discard outer husk on corn. Pick off any strands of "silk" remaining on ear of corn. Wash corn under cold water.

STEP 2: Put cold water in pan to 1 inch deep. Turn heat to high and bring water to boiling.

STEP 3: Lay corn in pan of boiling water. (If corn is too long, break so that corn lies flat in pan.) Cover pan and steam on high heat 5 minutes. Carefully remove corn. Spread hot corn with butter, salt, and pepper.

When buying corn, peel back husk and look for white or pale-yellow corn. Dark-gold corn can be tough when cooked.

CREAMED SPINACH

10 Minutes
Serves 1

NEED:

½ 10-ounce package frozen chopped SPINACH (cooked according to directions on package)

2 tablespoons SOUR CREAM

½ of 5-ounce can sliced WATER CHESTNUTS, drained (refrigerate the rest and use in a salad for another meal)

SALT, PEPPER to taste

STEP 1: Drain the cooked spinach well, squishing water out with fork.

STEP 2: Dump into small bowl and mix with sour cream.

STEP 3: Add water chestnuts, salt and pepper to taste.

Fabulous served over hot baked potato.

Simply
Veggies

Saucepan

Small Bowl

Top of Stove

MOM'S MASHED POTATOES

25 Minutes

Serves 1–2

Simply
Veggies

Saucepan With Lid

Top of Stove

Medium Heat

NEED:
2 POTATOES (white, red, or russet will do)
BUTTER or MARGARINE
MILK
SALT, PEPPER to taste

STEP 1: Wash and peel potatoes. Cut into quarters. Place in large saucepan. Cover with cold water. Cover with lid and cook on medium heat 20 minutes or till potatoes fall apart when you poke them with fork.

STEP 2: Remove from heat and drain potatoes in pan using lid to keep potatoes from falling out of pan. Set pan on counter and mash potatoes with fork (or, even better, with an electric mixer if you have one). Add a couple of pats of butter and about 2 tablespoons milk. Keep beating with fork or mixer till potatoes are light and fluffy. Salt and pepper to taste. Top with pat of butter.

NEED:

6 fresh MUSHROOMS, sliced or whole
1 tablespoon BUTTER or MARGARINE
juice from ½ LEMON
splash WHITE WINE
sprinkling of grated PARMESAN CHEESE

STEP 1: In skillet, on medium high heat, melt butter or margarine.
STEP 2: Add mushrooms, stir, and cook about 3 minutes, or until mushrooms start to brown.
STEP 3: Add lemon juice and wine. Stir and cook 2 minutes.
STEP 4: Remove from stove. Sprinkle with Parmesan cheese when ready to eat.

Great to use for a mushroom burger!!

5 Minutes
Serves 1

Simply Veggies

Skillet
Top of Stove
Medium High Heat

SPINACH & RICE WITH LEMON SAUCE

....

30 Minutes
Serves 1–2

Simply Veggies

Saucepan With Lid
Small Pan
Top of Stove

NEED:
½ cup WHITE RICE (not instant type)
½ cup fresh SPINACH, cut into strips
2 tablespoons OLIVE or VEGETABLE OIL
2 tablespoons BUTTER or MARGARINE
juice of ½ LEMON
1 sprig FRESH PARSLEY LEAVES, cut into small bits
SALT, PEPPER, to taste

STEP 1: Cook rice according to package instructions, but add spinach during the last 3 minutes of cooking by sprinkling it over rice. Cover and continue cooking rice.

STEP 2: In a small pan, melt butter on medium heat. Add lemon juice, parsley, salt, and pepper. Stir and heat.

STEP 3: When ready to serve rice, toss rice gently to mix in spinach and pour heated sauce over.

This is absolutely delicious and easy to make. Tastes great with fish.

STEAMY BROCCOLI

....

5 Minutes
Serves 1–2

NEED:
1 bunch BROCCOLI, cut into small florets
1 tablespoon BUTTER or MARGARINE
LEMON JUICE
sprinkling of DRIED HERBS (BASIL, TARRAGON, PARSLEY, or MARJO-
RAM)

STEP 1: Fill saucepan with 1 inch of salted water and bring to boil on high heat.
STEP 2: Add broccoli florets and let come to a boil again, then cover pan. Steam for 3 minutes or just until crisp-tender. Drain.
STEP 3: In same pan, add butter, lemon juice, and herbs. Toss with broccoli.

This great basic recipe works with most any vegetable, but softer textured vegetables, like squash, cook even faster.

Simply Veggies

Saucepan With Lid
Top of Stove
High Heat

TOMATO MUSHROOM SKILLET

10 Minutes
Serves 1

Simply Veggies

Skillet
Top of Stove
Medium High to
Medium Heat

NEED:
1 tablespoon OLIVE or VEGETABLE OIL
2 whole TOMATOES, sliced in half crosswise
6 MUSHROOMS, washed and sliced
GARLIC SALT
sprinkle of grated PARMESAN CHEESE

STEP 1: In skillet, heat oil on medium high heat for about 1 minute.
STEP 2: Lay tomato halves cut side down into skillet and dump mushrooms around tomatoes. Turn heat to medium and cook 3 minutes.
STEP 3: Turn tomatoes over and gently stir mushrooms. Sprinkle with garlic salt and Parmesan cheese.
STEP 4: Cook until tomatoes are hot and mushrooms are browned.

For a complete meal serve with eggs and toast, cooked the way you like them.

NEED:

   1 large BAKING POTATO (RUSSET POTATO is best choice)
   pat of MARGARINE or BUTTER
   splash MILK
   1 tablespoon softened or whipped CREAM CHEESE
   couple shakes grated PARMESAN CHEESE

BAKING POTATO

Preheat oven to 350°.

STEP 1: Pierce outside of potato with a fork about 4–5 times. Rub potato with small amount of butter or margarine. Bake in 350° oven for 45 minutes or until potato is soft to the touch.

FILLING

STEP 1: Cut baked potato in half lengthwise. Scoop out potato skin. (Do not cut through the bottom of potato skin.)

STEP 2: Place filling in small mixing bowl. Add butter, milk, and cream cheese. Stir with fork until soft and fluffy.

STEP 3: Return filling to potato skin. Set stuffed potatoes on sheet of foil. Sprinkle with Parmesan cheese.

STEP 4: Set oven temperature to Broil. Place potatoes under broiler for 2 minutes or until browned on top.

TWICE-BAKED POTATO

1 Hour
Serves 1

Simply
Veggies

Small Mixing Bowl

Aluminum Foil

350° Oven

Broiler

Handy Hint

Buy a quantity of bell peppers when they are in season and freeze them:
Remove the crown, stem, and seeds and place each pepper in a tightly sealed
plastic bag and freeze. They will keep for months, but use only for cooking after
freezing peppers, as they will lose their crispness.

SAUCES & SALSAS

2 Minutes
Serves 1

NEED:
½ teaspoon INSTANT CHICKEN BOUILLON (in soup section of market)
¼ cup HOT WATER
splash SOY SAUCE
1 teaspoon CORNSTARCH (in baking section of market)

STEP 1: In small cup or bowl, dissolve bouillon in hot water.
STEP 2: Add rest of ingredients. Stir.
STEP 3: Pour over hot stir-fried vegetables. Cook and stir on high heat 1
minute or till sauce thickens.

If you like a thicker sauce, add more cornstarch.

Sauces &
Salsas

Small Bowl
High Heat

Big D Salsa

5 Minutes
Makes 1 Quart

Sauces & Salsas

Large Bowl
No Cooking

NEED:
1 15-ounce can TOMATOES, cut up (not Italian style)
1 15-ounce can thick chunky TOMATO SAUCE
1 fresh TOMATO, chopped small
1 ONION, chopped
½ GREEN BELL PEPPER, chopped
1 clove GARLIC, mashed (or garlic salt)
1 teaspoon fresh JALAPEÑO PEPPER, chopped very fine (use according to taste)

Dump all ingredients in a large bowl. Stir to mix well. Cover and place in refrigerator.

Tastes best when allowed to chill for a few hours to let flavors blend.

NEED:
   1 can WHITE SAUCE (in soup or condiment section of market)
   handful CHEDDAR CHEESE, grated
   2 HARD-COOKED EGGS, chopped

In saucepan, on medium low heat, stir and heat white sauce and cheese till cheese melts. Add eggs. Stir and use.

USES:
   Serve over NOODLES, VEGETABLES or MEAT
   TOAST, slice of HAM, top with EZ Cheese Sauce
   Omit the eggs and use over omelets

EZ Cheese Sauce

....

5 Minutes
Several Servings

Sauces & Salsas

Saucepan
Top of Stove
Medium Low Heat

FRESH FRUIT DIPPING SAUCE

3 Minutes
Several Servings

Sauces & Salsas

Small Bowl
No Cooking

Blend in small bowl:
  2 spoonfuls BROWN SUGAR
  8-ounce carton SOUR CREAM

Use as a dip for fresh fruit:
  WATERMELON CHUNKS
  STRAWBERRIES
  BANANA CHUNKS
  PINEAPPLE SPEARS
  APPLE WEDGES
  PEAR SLICES

NEED:

½ cup SOY SAUCE
½ cup SUGAR
1 clove GARLIC
½ teaspoon GROUND GINGER (in spice section of market)

STEP 1: In saucepan, on medium heat, combine soy sauce and sugar. Stir and heat till sugar is dissolved.

STEP 2: Mash garlic clove with bottom of flat glass. Add garlic and ginger to sauce. Bring sauce to a boil. Remove from heat and let stand till just warm.

Use to marinate (soak) meat or vegetables 10 minutes before cooking, or brush on during cooking.

GREG'S HAWAIIAN TERIYAKI SAUCE

5 Minutes
Several Servings

Sauces & Salsas

Saucepan
Top of Stove
Medium Heat

HOMEMADE PESTO SAUCE

5 Minutes
Serves 1–2

Sauces & Salsas

Small Bowl
No Cooking

NEED:

½ cup fresh PARSLEY, chopped fine and packed in cup
1 tablespoon DRIED BASIL
½ teaspoon SALT
dash PEPPER
4 cloves GARLIC (remove outer skin and crush well)
⅓ cup OLIVE OIL
1 tablespoon MARGARINE
1 tablespoon BOILING WATER
½ cup grated PARMESAN CHEESE
¼ cup PINE NUTS (or walnuts), finely chopped

½ pound hot cooked PASTA

STEP 1: In small bowl, combine all ingredients except pasta.
STEP 2: Stir well with fork to blend flavors.
STEP 3: Pour sauce (it will be thick) over hot pasta and toss well to coat thoroughly.

FANTASTIC!!

NEED:
- ¼ cup PEANUT BUTTER
- ¼ cup WATER
- 1 tablespoon SOY SAUCE
- couple shakes GARLIC POWDER
- 2 tablespoons VINEGAR
- few sprinkles of dried CRUSHED RED PEPPER (use to taste)
- couple shakes POWDERED GINGER (optional)

STEP 1: In small saucepan, on medium heat, stir together peanut butter and water. Heat just until starts to bubble, then TURN HEAT OFF.

STEP 2: Add rest of ingredients and stir to blend flavors.

Serve over brown rice and top with Steamy Broccoli (page 123).

5 Minutes

Serves 1

Sauces & Salsas

Small Saucepan

Top of Stove

Medium Heat

SWEET & SPICY MUSTARD SAUCE

2 Minutes
Makes ¼ Cup

Sauces &
Salsas

Small Mixing Bowl

No Cooking

NEED:
½ cup HONEY
3 tablespoons SPICY HOT MUSTARD

STEP 1: In small mixing bowl, blend mustard into honey and stir well. Refrigerate until ready to use. Keeps 1 week.

Use as a dipping sauce with Chicken Bites (page 152).

MUSHROOMS—2-ounce can, drained and lightly cooked in 1 tablespoon margarine

LEMON BUTTER—squeeze ½ lemon into 1 tablespoon hot melted margarine

CHEDDAR CHEESE—grated over hot vegetables

EASY HOLLANDAISE—cook in small saucepan, on low heat:
    2 spoonfuls SOUR CREAM
    2 spoonfuls MAYONNAISE
    dab MUSTARD
    1 spoonful LEMON JUICE

TANGY SAUCE—stir together and pour over vegetables:
    1 tablespoon hot MARGARINE
    1 teaspoon MUSTARD
    squirt WORCESTERSHIRE SAUCE
    squirt LEMON JUICE

Sauces & Salsas

Misc. Utensils

Handy Hint

Reheating meats will be faster and you will save your pans from burning if you add a small amount of water (¼ cup) to pan first. Then add meat, cover, and heat on medium heat until hot.

❖

If meat has been defrosted, *don't refreeze* it unless it has been cooked.

❖

Add a spoonful of maple syrup for a great taste treat when heating leftover cooked squash or carrots.

USING LEFTOVERS

Using Leftovers:

Recipes Used Throughout This Cookbook

Beef—use in:

"Anything Goes" Fritatta—page 143

EZ Homemade Pot Pie—page 145

Quick Minestrone Soup—page 24

Yesterday's Roast Beef—page 147

Bread—use in:

Extra Pancakes (hint)—page 42

French Dipped Cheese Sandwich—page 12

French Toast—page 5

Tuna Soufflé—page 93

Chicken or Turkey—use in:

All in One Casserole—page 142

"Anything Goes" Fritatta—page 143

Everyone's Favorite Quesadillas—page 45

EZ Homemade Pot Pie—page 145

Quick Minestrone Soup—page 24

Ham or Pork—use in:

All in One Casserole—page 142

"Anything Goes" Fritatta—page 143

Everyone's Favorite Quesadillas—page 45

EZ Homemade Pot Pie—page 145

French Dipped Cheese Sandwich—page 12

Omelet Fillings—page 6

Rice and Pasta—use in:

Pasta Salad—page 34

Reheating Macaroni, Rice, or Pasta—page 146

Vegetables—use in:

All in One Casserole—page 142

"Anything Goes" Fritatta—page 143

EZ Homemade Pot Pie—page 145

Quick Minestrone Soup—page 24

ALL IN ONE CASSEROLE

40 Minutes
Serves 2–3

Using Leftovers

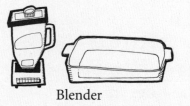

Blender
Ovenproof Baking Dish
375° Oven

NEED:

1 cup CHEDDAR CHEESE, shredded
1 small package FROZEN CHOPPED SPINACH, thawed (or any leftover cooked green vegetable)
1 ONION, chopped
1 cup cooked HAM or CHICKEN, cut in small pieces (or you can use canned tuna, shrimp, crab, chicken, etc., drained well)
1½ cups MILK
¾ cup BAKING MIX (Bisquick)
3 EGGS
½ teaspoon SALT, dash PEPPER

Preheat oven to 375°.

STEP 1: Squeeze all liquid out of spinach and lay spinach in bottom of shallow baking dish. Top with layer of meat, onion, then cheese.
STEP 2: Combine in blender jar milk, baking mix, eggs, salt, and pepper. Blend on medium speed 1 minute. Pour over layered casserole.
STEP 3: Bake in 375° oven 30 to 40 minutes (or till knife inserted comes out dry). Remove and let cool for a few minutes.

This makes enough to have next day. Even tastes good cold.

NEED:

3 EGGS
splash MILK
pinch herbs: BASIL, TARRAGON, PARSLEY, or MARJORAM
2 tablespoons BUTTER or MARGARINE
4 small CHERRY TOMATOES or 1 cut-up TOMATO
1 cup cooked VEGETABLES, MEAT, or CHICKEN,
cut up into bite-size pieces
Handful shredded PARMESAN, CHEDDAR, or JACK CHEESE

STEP 1: In small bowl or cup, beat eggs with milk and herbs. In skillet on medium high heat, melt butter and stir in egg mixture. Cook just until eggs start to firm up.

STEP 2: Add tomatoes, vegetables, meat, pasta, or whatever leftovers you want to use. Stir gently. Sprinkle with shredded cheese.

STEP 3: Cover and cook 10 minutes or until eggs are set and puffy.

"ANYTHING GOES" FRITATTA

....

10 Minutes
Serves 1

Using Leftovers

Skillet With Lid
Top of Stove
Medium High Heat

"Dump It In" and "Stir It Up" Basic Recipe for Leftovers

15 Minutes
Serves 1

Using Leftovers

Skillet With Lid

Top of Stove

High to Medium Low Heat

NEED:

2 tablespoons OLIVE or VEGETABLE OIL
½ ONION, sliced thinly or chopped small
½ BELL PEPPER, sliced into thin strips or chopped small
4 MUSHROOMS, sliced
1 TOMATO, chopped
couple squirts SOY SAUCE or TERIYAKI SAUCE
couple plops of CATSUP
1 cup of COOKED MEAT or CHICKEN, cut into bite-size pieces

STEP 1: In skillet, heat oil on high heat 1 minute. Add onion, bell pepper, and mushrooms. Stir and cook 3 minutes or until onion is limp.

STEP 2: Stir in tomato, sauces, and leftover cooked meat or chicken.

STEP 3: Turn heat to medium low. Cover and heat about 10 minutes or until everything is hot.

The key to this simple meal is making sure it is not too dry. Add a little water or red wine to get the sauce to the consistency you like.

NEED:
- dab of MARGARINE
- 1 10-ounce can CREAM OF CHICKEN SOUP
- 1 cup COOKED MEAT, cut into bite-size pieces
- 1–2 cups COOKED or FROZEN VEGETABLES
- ½ cup MILK
- 1 EGG
- 1 cup BAKING MIX (Bisquick)
- handful shredded CHEDDAR CHEESE

STEP 1: Rub bottom of pie pan with dab of margarine.

STEP 2: Spoon undiluted soup over bottom of pie pan. Put meat and vegetables on top of soup.

STEP 3: In small bowl, using a fork, mix together milk, egg, and baking mix. Batter will be lightly lumpy.

STEP 4: Spoon batter mixture over pie. Sprinkle batter with cheddar cheese.

STEP 5: Bake in 400° oven for 30–35 minutes or until top is golden and gravy is bubbly around edges. Cool 10 minutes before eating.

EZ HOMEMADE POT PIE

35 Minutes
Several Servings

Using Leftovers

Small Mixing Bowl
9-Inch Pie Pan
400° Oven

REHEATING MACARONI, RICE, OR PASTA

---

5 Minutes
Any Number of Servings

Using Leftovers

Saucepan With Lid
Top of Stove
Medium Heat

STEP 1: Dump leftover cooked macaroni, rice, or pasta into saucepan.

STEP 2: Add couple spoonfuls water. Cover tightly. Heat on medium heat a couple of minutes or till hot.

STEP 3: Drain off any excess water, then use.

NEED:

½ ONION, chopped
1 tablespoon MARGARINE
1 tablespoon FLOUR
1 cup BEEF BROTH (use INSTANT BEEF BOUILLON,
dissolved in hot water)
½ cup RED WINE
couple shakes WORCESTERSHIRE SAUCE
4 slices leftover cooked ROAST BEEF

STEP 1: In skillet, on medium heat, cook onion in margarine till golden.
Quickly stir in flour. Reduce heat to low.
STEP 2: Add beef broth to skillet slowly. Stir till well mixed with flour and
onion. Stir in wine and Worcestershire Sauce.
STEP 3: Lay beef slices in sauce and heat thoroughly (approximately 5 min-
utes).

YESTERDAY'S ROAST BEEF

10 Minutes
Serves 1–2

Using Leftovers

Skillet
Top of Stove
Medium to Low Heat

HANDY HINT

Enjoying your party too much? Forgot what's cooking on the stove? *Burned pots and pans?* Clean up a burned pan by filling it halfway with water and adding a squirt of dishwashing liquid. Boil it on the stove for several minutes. Burned parts will then rinse out easily.

Snacks & Party Foods

CHEESE FONDUE

....

5 Minutes
Several Servings

NEED:
- 2 tablespoons MARGARINE
- 2 tablespoons FLOUR
- 1 cup MILK
- 1 teaspoon MUSTARD
- 2 handfuls shredded CHEDDAR CHEESE
- FRENCH BREAD, cut into bite-size chunks

STEP 1: In saucepan, on medium low heat, melt margarine and stir in flour till well mixed and smooth.

STEP 2: Slowly add milk. Stir and heat till thick. Add mustard and cheese, stirring till melted.

Dip chunks of French bread into cheese sauce using forks or chopsticks.

Snacks & Party Foods

Saucepan
Top of Stove
Medium Low Heat

CHICKEN BITES

20 Minutes
Several Servings

Snacks & Party Foods

Skillet, Small Bowl,
Shallow Dish
Top of Stove
High Heat

NEED:
4 skinless, boneless CHICKEN BREASTS, cut into 1-inch cubes
½ cup MILK (poured into small bowl)
½ cup FLOUR
couple shakes each: BLACK PEPPER, SALT, PAPRIKA
½ cup VEGETABLE OIL

STEP 1: In small shallow pie plate or dish, mix together flour and seasonings.
STEP 2: Heat oil in skillet on high heat until very hot.
STEP 3: Dip chicken into milk and then into flour mixture.
STEP 4: Carefully lay chicken into hot oil. Turn and cook until golden brown and crispy all over. Drain on paper towel.

*Dip chicken bites into store-bought Ranch Dressing
or homemade Sweet & Spicy Mustard Sauce (page 36).*

NEED:

   1 container refrigerated PIZZA CRUST
   2 tablespoons OLIVE OIL
   3 cloves GARLIC, cut into small pieces
   couple pinches ITALIAN HERBS
   1–2 TOMATOES, sliced thinly
   ¼ ONION, sliced thinly
   ¼ cup grated PARMESAN or ROMANO CHEESE

STEP 1: Open container of pizza crust, unroll, and spread onto flat baking sheet.
STEP 2: In small bowl or cup, combine olive oil, garlic, and herbs. Drizzle over pizza crust.
STEP 3: Top with tomato and onion slices and sprinkle with cheese.
STEP 4: Bake in 425° oven for 15 minutes or until crust and cheese are golden in color.

Don't overcrowd tomato and onion slices—spread them around sparingly.
This is not pizza, it is really Italian flat bread.

FOCACCIA

20 Minutes
Several Servings

Snacks & Party Foods

Baking Sheet
425° Oven

GARLIC CHEDDAR CHEESE BREAD

....

5 Minutes
Serves 1

Snacks & Party Foods

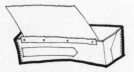

Aluminum Foil
Oven, Set to "Broil"

NEED:
2 SOURDOUGH or FRENCH ROLLS, sliced lengthwise
2 tablespoons BUTTER or MARGARINE
2 cloves GARLIC, mashed or cut into tiny pieces
handful shredded CHEDDAR CHEESE

STEP 1: Butter cut sides of rolls.
STEP 2: Sprinkle buttered rolls with garlic and top with cheese.
STEP 3: Place on sheet of aluminum foil and put under broiler.
STEP 4: Broil 1–2 minutes or until cheese is bubbly.

NEED:

    1 8-ounce can CRUSHED PINEAPPLE, drained well
    1 4-ounce container whipped CREAM CHEESE, room temperature
    couple leaves FRESH MINT, cut into small pieces
    12 FLOUR TORTILLAS

STEP 1: In small bowl, place drained pineapple. Squish out excess liquid with fork and drain off.

STEP 2: Add cream cheese and stir to blend well.

STEP 3: Fill middle of flat tortilla with a spoonful of mixture. Sprinkle with a few of the mint leaves. Fold in edges and roll up tightly. Continue until all tortillas are filled.

STEP 4: Wrap tortillas in plastic wrap or aluminum foil and refrigerate until ready to use.

STEP 5: When ready to use, remove from foil or plastic wrap and slice each wrap into 6–8 slices.

Snacks & Party Foods

Small Bowl

Aluminum Foil or Plastic Wrap

No Cooking

Hot Clams & Cheese

10 Minutes
Several Servings

**Snacks &
Party Foods**

Saucepan

Top of Stove

Low Heat

NEED:

1 8-ounce jar PROCESSED CHEESE SPREAD
4 GREEN ONIONS, finely chopped
½ GREEN BELL PEPPER, finely chopped
dash PAPRIKA (in spice section of market)
1 tablespoon WORCESTERSHIRE SAUCE
1 7-ounce can minced CLAMS, drained well

In saucepan, on low heat, mix all ingredients together. Stir and heat till cheese melts.

USES:

Fantastic as a sauce over linguini pasta
Serve hot with chips
Dunk bite-size pieces of French bread

DILL DIP

NEED:

    1 cup MAYONNAISE
    1 8-ounce carton SOUR CREAM
    2 GREEN ONIONS, sliced thin
    1½ teaspoons DILL WEED (in spice section of market)
    1½ teaspoons SEASONED SALT

Blend all together in bowl and chill. Serve with raw vegetables.

DEVILISH DIP

NEED:

    1 8-ounce carton SOUR CREAM
    4¼-ounce can DEVILED HAM SPREAD
    dash WORCESTERSHIRE SAUCE

Blend together and chill.

3 Minutes
Several Servings

Snacks & Party Foods

Small Bowl

No Cooking

Patty's Deviled Eggs

10 Minutes
Several Servings

Snacks & Party Foods

Small Bowl
No Cooking

NEED:
6 HARD-COOKED EGGS
2 tablespoons MAYONNAISE
½ teaspoon MUSTARD
couple dashes each CELERY SALT, GARLIC SALT, PEPPER
1 small can BABY SHRIMP (optional but sure tastes good)
PARSLEY and PAPRIKA (optional)

STEP 1: Cut eggs in half, lengthwise. Scoop out yolks (yellow part) and put in small mixing bowl. (Put white halves aside to be filled later.) Add mayonnaise, mustard, celery salt, garlic salt, and pepper to yolks. Mash and stir together till everything is well mixed, smooth, and creamy.

STEP 2: If using shrimp, stir very gently into mixture.

STEP 3: Spoon mixture into egg-white halves. Sprinkle tops of yolks with paprika and parsley. Lay on attractive platter and place in refrigerator till time to serve.

Better hide them with aluminum foil or they may just disappear before your party.

NEED:
   1 can refrigerated CRESCENT ROLLS
   1 package SAUSAGE LINKS (brown-and-serve type, skinless)

Preheat oven to 350°.

STEP 1: Cook sausages according to directions on package. Remove sausages and drain on paper towel.

STEP 2: Roll sausages into uncooked crescent rolls, follow directions for rolling on package. Place on cookie sheet or aluminum foil and bake in 350° oven 10 minutes or till golden.

PIGS IN A BLANKET

15 Minutes
Makes 8 Small Rolls

Snacks & Party Foods

Skillet
Aluminum Foil
350° Oven

Saucy Barbecued Franks

8 Minutes
Several Servings

Snacks & Party Foods

Skillet
Top of Stove
Medium to Low Heat

NEED:
¼ ONION, chopped
1 tablespoon MARGARINE
⅛ GREEN BELL PEPPER, chopped
½ can TOMATO SOUP
1 tablespoon BROWN SUGAR
dash WORCESTERSHIRE SAUCE
quick dash VINEGAR
dab MUSTARD
4–5 WIENERS, cut into bite-size pieces

STEP 1: In skillet, on medium heat, cook onion in margarine till onion is transparent.
STEP 2: Dump in other ingredients, except wieners. Stir well to blend flavors.
STEP 3: Add wieners and heat on low heat 2 minutes or till wieners are hot.

Serve in a heatproof dish and set on a hot plate.
Be sure to have toothpicks nearby for skewers.

NEED:
2 EGGS, lightly beaten with fork
1 tablespoon MARGARINE
spoonful grated CHEDDAR CHEESE
½ ONION, finely chopped
spoonful BARBECUE SAUCE
large FLOUR TORTILLA

STEP 1: In skillet, on medium heat, melt margarine. Cook and stir eggs till almost done to your liking. Add cheese and onion. Gently stir and cook 1 minute. Remove to plate.

STEP 2: Quickly heat tortilla on dry hot skillet. (Watch, don't burn.)

STEP 3: Spread egg mixture on tortilla. Spoon barbecue sauce over and fold up, burrito style.

....

10 Minutes
Serves 1

Snacks & Party Foods ▶

Skillet
Top of Stove
Medium Heat

HANDY HINT

Quickie cookie: Lay a marshmallow on a graham cracker.
Set on a sheet of aluminum foil. Heat under broiler just until marshmallow
melts and gets brown and bubbly.

❖

To make toasted nuts: Spread them in a baking pan and bake at
350° for 10 minutes, stirring once, or until golden.

DESSERTS

···

3 Minutes
Serves 1

NEED:
PEAR HALF
VANILLA ICE CREAM or FROZEN YOGURT
CHOCOLATE TOPPING

STEP 1: Place a pear half in bottom of small glass bowl.
STEP 2: Top with ice cream or frozen yogurt.
STEP 3: Drizzle hot or cold chocolate topping over.

Try same recipe using VANILLA ICE CREAM or YOGURT and:
PEACHES and BUTTERSCOTCH TOPPING
HALVED BANANA and PINEAPPLE TOPPING
HALF CANTALOUPE and spoonful BROWN SUGAR

Desserts

Small Serving Dish

No Cooking

Healthy Candy

10 Minutes
Makes 18 to 20 1-Inch Balls

Desserts

Bowl
No Cooking

NEED:
   ½ cup PEANUT BUTTER
   ½ cup HONEY
   1 cup WHEAT GERM
   shredded COCONUT or chopped NUTS

STEP 1: In bowl, blend peanut butter, honey, and wheat germ together. Roll into small balls.
STEP 2: Roll balls in coconut or nuts. Refrigerate.

Eat when chilled and hardened.

To keep candy from sticking to your hands, rub a little butter on your fingers first.

NEED:

    1 small box LEMON or LIME SUGAR-FREE GELATIN
    ¾ cup BOILING WATER
    12 ICE CUBES
    1 cup LOW-CAL WHIPPED TOPPING, softened to room temperature
    several thin slices of fresh LIMES or LEMONS
    1 8-inch PIE CRUST, baked and cooled (try the frozen ones—they're great)

STEP 1: In large mixing bowl, add boiling water to gelatin mix and stir 2 minutes. Add ice cubes, one at a time, and stir another 2 minutes. Gelatin should be starting to thicken.

STEP 2: Gently stir in whipped topping. Stir till well blended and smooth. Pour into baked and cooled pie crust. Refrigerate for several hours before cutting.

Fancy it up by adding thin lemon slices on top of pie before serving.

Low-Cal Cool Pie

10 Minutes
Several Servings

Desserts

Large Mixing Bowl
No Cooking

Mom's Nut Bread

1 Hour
Several Servings

Desserts

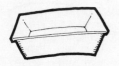

Small Loaf Pan
350° Oven

NEED:
- ¾ cup BROWN SUGAR
- 2 cups FLOUR
- 3 teaspoons BAKING POWDER
- ¾ cup chopped WALNUTS
- 1 EGG
- 2 teaspoons SALT
- 1 cup MILK
- 1 teaspoon OIL or MARGARINE (to grease loaf pan)

Preheat oven to 350°.

STEP 1: Dump all ingredients into mixing bowl and mix with wooden spoon till large lumps are gone.

STEP 2: Spoon into a greased loaf pan and bake in 350° oven about 50 minutes or till golden brown.

STEP 3: Remove from oven and set on wire rack (if you don't have a wire rack, use a couple of knives laid flat). Let cool before slicing.

Fabulous spread with margarine or cream cheese.

NEED:

   2 cups SUGAR
   ⅔ cup MILK
   6 tablespoons PEANUT BUTTER
   1 teaspoon VANILLA FLAVORING EXTRACT (in spice section of market)
   ¼ pound SALTINE SODA CRACKERS (about 40 single crackers crushed into fine crumb texture)

STEP 1: In small saucepan, stir together sugar and milk. Turn heat to medium and stir until mixture starts to boil. Cook and stir 3 minutes.

STEP 2: Add peanut butter and vanilla. Stir to mix well.

STEP 3: Stir in crushed saltine crackers.

STEP 4: Press onto cookie sheet until firm and flat. Let sit 30 minutes and then cut into squares.

Quick tip to crush crackers: Place crackers in a large plastic bag and crush with rolling pin, heavy skillet, or wooden kitchen hammer . . . or use a blender.

No-Bake Peanut Butter Cookies

10 Minutes
Makes 2 Dozen

Desserts

Small Saucepan

Cookie Sheet

Top of Stove

Medium Heat

No-Mix Peach Cobbler

....

45 Minutes
Several Servings

Desserts

13-Inch-by-9-Inch Oven
Baking Dish
350° Oven

NEED:
    2 16-ounce cans sliced PEACHES with juice
    1 package YELLOW CAKE MIX
    1 stick MARGARINE (or ½ cup)
    1 cup chopped NUTS

STEP 1: Spread peaches and juice in bottom of baking dish.
STEP 2: Sprinkle dry cake mix on top of peaches. Dot with margarine.
        Sprinkle nuts on top.
STEP 3: Bake 45 minutes in 350° oven or till cobbler is golden.

Serve warm with ice cream.

NEED:
    Unsliced FRESH BREAD (best if fresh from a bakery)
    BUTTER or MARGARINE
    GRANULATED SUGAR
    LEMON CURD (this is the stuff used as cake fillings) or RED BERRY JAM

STEP 1: Slice fresh bread and spread liberally with butter.
STEP 2: Sprinkle sugar over and shake off excess.
STEP 3: Spread on lemon curd or jam.

Now, slice in quarters, put on a pretty plate, sit down with a cold glass of milk and enjoy. Yum!!

Poor Folks' Cake

....

1 Minute
Several Servings

Desserts

Sharp Knife
No Cooking

QUICK BAKED APPLES

20 Minutes
Serves 1–2

Desserts

Saucepan With Lid
Top of Stove
Medium to Low Heat

NEED:

2 large BAKING APPLES (MACINTOSH, ROME BEAUTY)
2 small spoonfuls SUGAR
dab MARGARINE
dash CINNAMON
½ cup WATER

STEP 1: Wash apples and scoop out cores (don't go through the bottom of the apples). In center hole of each apple, pour sugar till almost full. Dab with margarine and sprinkle cinnamon on top.
STEP 2: Pour water in saucepan. Gently place apples in water. Cover.
STEP 3: Turn heat to medium and bring water to boiling point. Lower heat and cook apples till tender (approximately 20 minutes).

Serve hot with warm milk or ice cream.

NEED:
    3-ounce package STRAWBERRY GELATIN
    ⅔ cup BOILING WATER
    14 ICE CUBES
    1 8-ounce carton small curd COTTAGE CHEESE
    1 BANANA, sliced
    GRAHAM CRACKER CRUST, premade (in baking mix section of market)

STEP 1: Dissolve gelatin in boiling water in large bowl. Stir 3 minutes. Add ice cubes and stir 2 more minutes. (Gelatin will be thick.) Remove excess ice cubes.

STEP 2: Add cottage cheese and stir well to blend.

STEP 3: Lay banana slices in bottom of pie crust. Spoon gelatin mix over bananas and chill 1 hour before cutting.

STRAWBERRY DELIGHT PIE

10 Minutes
6 Slices

Desserts

Large Bowl
Pie Plate
No Cooking

SUGARED WALNUT ICE CREAM SUNDAES

3 Minutes
Serves 1

Desserts

Small Saucepan

Ice Cream Dish

Top of Stove

Medium Heat

NEED:

1 tablespoon BUTTER
1 cup WALNUT HALVES
¼ cup MAPLE FLAVORED PANCAKE SYRUP
VANILLA ICE CREAM

STEP 1: In saucepan, over medium heat, melt butter. Add walnuts. Stir and cook 1 minute.

STEP 2: Add pancake syrup. Cook and stir until walnuts are coated and hot.

STEP 3: Place ice cream into serving dish and top with hot walnuts.

NEED:
    PACKAGED PANCAKE MIX (Bisquick)
    SOUR CREAM or COTTAGE CHEESE
    BERRIES, fresh, frozen (thawed) or canned (drained)
    couple spoonfuls GRANULATED SUGAR

STEP 1: Using directions on package, prepare thin pancakes. Cook as directed making 2 or 3 large-size pancakes, being careful when you turn them. Set cooked pancakes on an attractive serving plate.
STEP 2: Spread spoonfuls of sour cream (or cottage cheese) along center of each pancake. Top with spoonful of berries and sprinkle of sugar.
STEP 3: Roll up each pancake and top with a few more berries, a small spoonful of sour cream (or cottage cheese), and small sprinkle of sugar.

Try this for a gorgeous dessert or impressive brunch!

What a Crepe

10 Minutes
Several Servings

Desserts

Skillet
Top of Stove
Medium High Heat

HANDY HINT

If you don't have a punch bowl, use the kitchen sink—*washed first, please*.
Club soda will shine up stainless steel sinks in a jiffy.

DRINKS

....

5 Minutes
Serves 12 (1 cup each)

NEED:

    2 6-ounce cans FROZEN ORANGE JUICE
    1 6-ounce can FROZEN LEMONADE
    1½ quarts ICE WATER
    2 quarts CHAMPAGNE (well chilled)
    ORANGE SLICES (chilled)

STEP 1: Dilute orange juice and lemonade with ice water in punch bowl.
STEP 2: Just before serving, gently pour champagne into punch bowl.
STEP 3: Float thin orange slices in bowl. Serve.

Just before serving, try adding 1 pint orange sherbet to punch.

Drinks

Punch Bowl
No Cooking

COFFEE MOCHA EUROPA

10 Minutes
Several Servings

Coffee Cups
Coffeemaker

NEED:
    brewed strong hot COFFEE
    HOT CHOCOLATE COCOA
    WHIPPED TOPPING
    FRESH ORANGE PEEL, grated

STEP 1: Stir together in large mugs equal amounts hot coffee and hot chocolate.
STEP 2: Top with whipped topping and sprinkle with grated orange peel.

QUICK COFFEE MOCHA

Just stir in a shot of chocolate syrup in place of hot chocolate cocoa to cup of steaming hot instant coffee. Top with sprinkle of cinnamon and plop of whipped cream.

....

5 Minutes
Several Servings

NEED:

   2 liters WHITE or RED WINE (chilled)
   1 quart APPLE JUICE
   juice of ¼ LEMON
   1 cup SUGAR
   1 quart GINGER ALE (chilled)
   ICE CUBES

STEP 1: Dump everything into a very large punch bowl, stirring to dissolve
       the sugar.
STEP 2: Add ice cubes and serve.

Drinks

If a large punch is not available, just scrub out the kitchen sink, plug it up, and use it. Just make sure you really clean it first.

Large Punch Bowl or
Large Leakproof Container
No Cooking

LEMON AIDE

....

2 Minutes
Serves 1

Drinks

Quart Jar With Lid
No Cooking

NEED:
QUART JAR with tight-fitting lid
CRUSHED ICE
½ LEMON
spoonful SUGAR or LOW-CAL SWEETENER

STEP 1: Fill jar ⅔ full with crushed ice. Add water almost to top of jar.
STEP 2: Squeeze lemon in. Sprinkle sugar on top.
STEP 3: Close lid tightly. Shake vigorously. Open and drink! Cool and refreshing!

NEED:
- COFFEE
- 7 whole CLOVES
- 1 stick CINNAMON
- 3 large spoonfuls SUGAR
- WHIPPED TOPPING

STEP 1: Before brewing six cups coffee in coffeemaker, add cloves, cinnamon, and sugar to dry coffee grounds in basket.

STEP 2: Perk coffee as usual. Pour in mugs.

STEP 3: Top off each mug of coffee with a plop of whipped topping.

VIENNESE COFFEE

10 Minutes
Serves 6

Drinks

Coffeemaker

INDEX

(continued)